ANA AL-HAQQ RECONSIDERED

Ana al-Haqq Reconsidered

With a Translation of *KITAB AL-TAWASIN*
by Husain b. Mansur Hallaj

by

GILANI KAMRAN

KITAB BHAVAN
New Delhi-110002

KITAB BHAVAN
Publishers, Distributors, Exporters & Importers
1784, Kalan Mahal, Darya Ganj,
New Delhi - 1100 02 (India)

Phones : +91-11-23277392, 23274686
Fax : (+91-11) 23263383
Mob. ✆ : +91-11-9953098606
Website : www.kitabbhavan.net

E-mail : info@kitabbhavan.net
:nasri@vsnl.com

Reprint : 2023

ISBN-10 : 81-7151-185-6
ISBN-13 : 978-81-7151-185-3

Book Code No. : A00146

Batch ID : SPRFN040223

Printed & Published in India by :
Moonis Ali Nasri for KITAB BHAVAN
1784, Kalan Mahal, Darya Ganj,
New Delhi - 1100 02 [India]

TO

IQBAL BEGUM

MY WIFE

AND

SEERAT

MY DAUGHTER

WITH DEEP AFFECTIONS

PREFACE

Ana al-Haqq has once again become a cry in the wilderness. Only the landscape has changed, and the world of Hallaj is replaced by the tensions of modern times. In the changed environment the Muslims are faced with a strange phenomenon: strange in the sense that it has no familiar counterpart in the recent history of Muslim creative thought. To my mind, therefore, the conditions of our times provide sufficient justification for a reconsideration of what Hallaj had to say in similar circumstances.

It is an agreed observation that the Muslim world is still at present passing through its Age of Faith; its sensibility is undissociated, and its human responses are still sensitive to physical and metaphysical affections. But the contact with the spirit of modern knowledge has much altered the intellectual scene of the Muslim world. The questions of modern knowledge have invaded the Age of Faith with the result that the Muslim mind has come across a challenge and a crisis. Man's alienation from his fundamental condition has appeared in the Muslim world as a major question, and much in fact depends on how this question is answered by us in the foreseeable future. Intellectually, the Muslim world appears to be placed in an unresolved situation and its pathos seems to gradually drift away from the Age of Faith towards a state of alienation. The creative thinking has discovered its sources on the alienated soil, and what is history is rapidly becoming a part of legend. This seems to be the crisis of the Muslim world in the present times. It is not reasonable, however, to describe all this as a movement towards modernism because what is happening is scarcely horizontal. What is, in fact, taking place is the transformation in terms of alienation. The contemporary poetry being written in the Muslim world would provide evidence for what I have suggested.

Nevertheless, what has suffered the most in this situational crisis is the metaphysical relationship which forms the basis of an age of Faith. Therefore, the dread of unknowability of God has appeared on the outer boundaries of the physical world, and in the absence of a firm metaphysical relationship the Revelation and its Truth is left out almost undefended.

It is against this background that I have attempted to approach Hallaj and his mystic thought because I feel that modern Muslim world shares much of its anguish with the Hallajian situation. I have tried to place Hallaj in his Age and have provided *Tawasin's* textual context to *ana al-haqq* in order to discover the common ground between the world past and the present. *Al-Haqq*, the Truth, though it possesses its traditional suggestions, has also acquired slightly changed dimensions in my interpretation. However, while moving about in the world of Hallaj I have realised that Hallaj is still alive and relevant to the historic phenomenon in which we, as Muslims, are at present involved. I think Hallaj can answer satisfactorily some of the fundamental questions which disturb us today.

Hallaj was never forgotten by us. He has permeated our folk imagination and has lived through the centuries in our individual and collective memory. Nevertheless, for modern Hallaj Studies the credit indeed goes to the Western scholars who have reintroduced him on the graph of our present-day creative thought. It was most surely their love for the best in human experience which, by way of Hallaj and their interest in Islamic mysticism, enabled the Muslim Renaissance to enter its creative phase in the modern world. With these feelings I have consulted them at various places in my present work. I hope that in the contemporary state of our creative thought Hallaj and his experience will help us in resolving the tensions which are of course the price of a nation's progress in history.

In the end, I take this opportunity to thank Mawlana Atiq-ur-Rehman of Government College, Rawalpindi, who very kindly translated into Urdu Hallaj's *Kitab al-Tawasin* for me, and helped me on various important points of textual interpretation. My thanks are also due to Professor Munawar Ashraf of M.A.O. College, who has been kind enough to go through the manuscript.

Gilani Kamran

TABLE OF CONTENTS

ANA AL-HAQQ RECONSIDERED

(1)

The mystic phrase *ana al-haqq* has a long history both as a statement and as an experience. As a statement it has been variously discussed and its pantheistic overtones have been either rejected or justified according to the shifting of viewpoints. As an experience its validity has frequently been challenged and at best exposed to serious doubt. In the framework supplied by the Muslim speculative thought the phrase *ana al-haqq* has held an important place in the relationship between God and man. But precisely for this reason the phrase has caused and can still cause embarrassment to the Muslim theological position because it suggests the interpenetration of the divine and the human nature within man. It is, therefore, that, in spite of the reverence given to him, Hallaj has been made to stay on the periphery of Muslim consciousness, and, perhaps for this, he has, in course of time, emerged as a very strong influence on the creative impluse in the Muslim world. However, the phrase *ana al-haqq* has throughout existed as an ambivalent expression with divided sympathies.

The *Kashf al-Mahjub* has been one of the earliest

authorities which has accepted and accommodated Hallaj within the tradition of Muslim creative thought. It has assessed Hallaj in terms of his spiritual background and has made an appreciable move towards the nature of his experience which forms the basis of the mystic phrase *ana al-haqq*. But *Kashf al-Mahjub* clearly demarcates the areas of responsibility between the experience and its expression. The experience at its unformed level seems quite agreeable and genuine, but its inner environment is dismissed as unreliable. Whatever be the nature of the experience, the content of its expression is considered to be an unwelcome description of the ecstatic state. "A person overcome with rapture has not the power of expressing himself correctly," says *Kashf al-Mahjub*. However, while discussing the nature of such expressions as *ana al-haqq*, the opinion about Hallaj becomes gradually sympathetic and the charge of pantheistic content of such expressions by Hallaj is emphatically ruled out. "Some orthodox theologians reject him [Hallaj] on the ground," says *Kashf al-Mahjub*, "that his [Hallaj's] sayings are pantheistic, but the offence lies solely in the expression, not in the meaning." With *Kashf al-Mahjub* the emphasis shifts from the underlying experience to the quality of its expression, and *ana al-haqq* is taken out of its ecstatic environment and placed within the structure of language.

In the value-framework of his age the verbal expression of Hallaj's ecstatic state existed as a totality, and the meaning of the expression rested on the biographical evidence and on the dimensions available within the ecstatic state. It was perhaps for this reason that the phrase *ana al-haqq* could not derive any other meaning except the one dictated by the academic discipline of the Divine Unity. Consequently, *al-Haqq* became synonymous with the Divinity, and the phrase *ana al-haqq* was understood to carry suggestions towards unification of God and man. Thus, "I am the Truth" became transformed to the startling expression of "I am God". However, in the first two hundred years of the controversy it was *Kashf al-Mahjub* which had attempted to strike a balance and had indicated that the expression could be made a subject of literary treatment.

The phrase *ana al-haqq* offers a direct Subject-Object relationship which exists within the auditory-visual dimension, where this relationship is completely dissolved into total loss of identity on the part of the human Subject. Thus the Object becomes the Subject, and the words spoken (*ana al-haqq*) are ascribed to that Subject (the other), though they are conveyed through the agency of the identity of the human Subject which is being withheld in its moment of time. In this lofty state of ecstatic power the Subject-Object relationship simply appears as a primary category of knowledge, and suddenly the relationship stands reversed. Only the voice is heard—"I am the Truth". Husain b. Mansur ceases to exist !

Ibn 'Arabi took up the problem of relationship in the context of ecstatic state and emphasised the central position of the personal "I" in the construction of the phrase. Thus, *ana*—"I" became the locus of ecstatic experience and *al-haqq* as Object entered the radius of its imaginal thought. It was held that God reveals Himself in five planes: (1) the plane of the Essence; (2) the plane of the Attributes; (3) the plane of the Actions; (4) the plane of Similitudes, and (5) the plane of Sensible Vision. Each of these was considered to be the copy of the one above it, so that whatever appeared in the Sensible World was the symbol of an unseen reality. In this perspective *the truth* reflected in the mystic phrase could only, by successive stages, represent the Divine Essence and even in the most intimate Subject-Object relationship the unitive state could formally exist in a pure representational condition. Regarded as such the content of the personal "I" was shown to hold an added dimension of imaginal thought within the ecstatic state. The power of ecstasy could become creative and purposeful when imaginal thought was activated by the ecstatic state. The personal "I" could receive the truth in its representational form only when all these faculties of the Subject co-ordinated in a single act of the will. The pantheistic nature of Hallaj's mystic phrase was thus made unconvincing in this scheme of knowledge.

This, however, led to another aspect of the Subject-Object relationship where the Object is equated with God. Without this aspect *al-haqq* would not yield its theomorphic meaning. The medium of the Burning Bush on the Sinai was incorporated in the argument for the implied theomorphic meaning. It was suggested that the Burning Bush had really appeared in response to Moses' search for the fire in the wilderness. Thus the search for the fire on the part of Moses became an underlying relationship between him and his desired object. Outwardly it was the search for the fire in the physical sense, but inwardly the search had its deeper spiritual dimension as well. The Burning Bush on the Sinai, therefore, became the medium for the theophanic vision as the physical and the spiritual dimension co-ordinated to establish an intimate relationship between God and Moses. And as a result of this relationship the Voice of God was heard by Moses.

This aspect of relationship raised an important question : What is the exact nature of the Burning Bush and of its identity with regard to the voice of God ? The Burning Bush was accepted as the medium and the voice of God was understood to have been heard by Moses from on high. Nevertheless, the literalists' viewpoint did not demarcate between the medium and the voice, and consequently the two were enlisted in speculative thought as a unitive act ; the medium supplied the form for the voice to be heard by Moses. In course of time this led to the assumption that the voice of God had actually spoken to Moses through the Burning Bush. The Object in its spiritual dimension had assumed a physical form to enter into dialogue with the Subject of its intimate relationship. Thinking along these lines naturally led to the doctrine of the Logos, and as a corollary the mystic phrase *ana al-haqq* became a heretical statement for the Muslims.

With this assumption, however, that the word of God had appeared within the framework of Subject-Object relationship, *ana al-haqq* ("I am the Truth") was accordingly interpreted to adjust it in the tradition of speculative thought. Shaikh Ahmad of Sirhind (1563-1624) discussed it within the canon of theological tradition and held that *ana al-haqq* was a situational statement and that it represented a quality of authentic experience. The Shaikh suggested that *ana*—the personal "I," and *al-haqq*, the Truth, had no reference to a unitive condition, in fact ; *al-haqq* completely surrounded the consciousness of the contemplative ego. Placed in this state the *ana* could only know the surrounding *al-haqq*—and simultaneously lose its own identity. It was in fact the loss of personal identity which gave significance to Hallaj's statement. The Shaikh held that *ana al-haqq* did not have any reference to unification either with the Divine Essence or its Attribute. Thus, *ana al-haqq*, as "I am the Truth," was categorically discarded by the Shaikh who interpreted the phrase as affirmation by negation. According to him, *ana al-haqq* did not carry the affirmatory meaning of "I am the Truth," but simply made the statement that "I am not, He only is". Without negation of the self, the affirmation of Divine Truth remains unresolved. Hallaj had in fact affirmed the faith through negation of the contemplative ego.

However, in the perspective suggested by the teachings of Shaikh Ahmad of Sirhind the contemplative ego which forms the active subject of *ana al-haqq* relationship does not undergo the transformations guided by the technical vocabulary of dissolution, or of merger into the Other. The "Other" as an ontological idea does not permit assimilation of the contemplative ego within its otherness. The Object remains the

Object, while the Subject in its contemplation is required to observe its presence. The contemplative ego can only participate in the knowledge of that presence. The Subject-Object relationship in its horizontal and vertical extension is supplemented by the value-framework in which the contemplative ego is placed with regard to the knowledge of the Divine Presence. The dimensional relationship is accordingly modified to agree to the changed speculative conditions. The ego and the Divine Presence relationship becomes concentric relationship between the circumference and the point located at the centre. Hallaj's *Tasin al-Da'irah* and *Tasin al-Nuqtah* support the view held by Shaikh Ahmad of Sirhind.

(2)

It seems appropriate, at this point, to place the phrase *ana al-haqq* in its contemporary intellectual setting in order to determine its relevance within its original milieu. Like all creative expressions, *ana al-haqq* keeps its roots in the intellectual history of the period and emerges as an image of the collective creative urge of its environment. However, it would be hardly fruitful to place it within one or the other tradition of thought which in retrospect seems to have been active in the Baghdad of that period. It was in fact the total intellectual situation—the World of the Mind, which appears to have discovered its orientation in the mystic Hallajian statement of *ana al-haqq*.

The intellectual life of the Muslim world between Hasan Basri (d. 728) and Mansur Hallaj (d. 922), though rich and continuous, was seriously surrounded by theological and philosophic questions. The religious sensibility which was compact and indivisible in the earlier days at Basrah had become increasingly less compact, and gradually the approach to faith and its truth inclined towards controversy. The rise of the Mu'tazilah, the philosophic investigations of Kindi (d. 873) and Farabi (d. 950), the theological debates and disputes, and the underlying quest of the human mind for its Maker, made the Truth relative and correspondingly weakened the efficacy of the available instruments of knowledge. Thus Reason, the effective instrument of human thought, lost much of its value when it reached the conclusion of the unknowability of God. The Mu'tazilah discovered a characterless identity of God through their keen sense of abstraction. Between them and al-Ash'ari (873-941), however, the faith and its truth moved from one form of affirmation to another, i.e. from logical construction to theological positivism. Yet it lacked the assurance of personal element. The intellectual life became increasingly richer with added dimensions of thought, but the individual personality under its impact fragmented into reason, revelation and faith. The co-ordination of reason and faith in favour of revelation remained unresolved. And a long series of questions covered the horizon of the intellectual scene for over a time-span of two hundred years.

It was in this climate of ideas that the Aristotelian argument leading back to the First Cause was modified to serve the requirements of Junaid's (d. 909) doctrine of the *Mithaq* : the doctrine based on the pre-natal covenant of the human soul. The series of successive causes, which formed the structure of Aristotelian argument, worked in the world of sense only and of course led to the First Cause, but the argument at its extreme point in time abruptly leaped from the world of sense into a world which escaped all measurement. The argument moved beyond the world of sense into another region which is independent of geometry of existence. It was this other region which appeared in Junaid's doctrine of the *Mithaq*. Thus, the combination of the two prepared the individual personality for the role to undertake quest for its Maker. Reason was abandoned in favour of experience.

It will, however, be an oversimplification to say that Reason was altogether discarded as an instrument of knowledge and that Experience was taken up as an exclusive guide even for the areas of the world of sense. What happened in fact was that Reason and Experience were integrated to blend into a better and more effective instrument of knowledge in order to cover the gradations of total reality. This new instrument of knowledge became the creative experience of Sufism.

The creative experience thus entered the intellectual perspective of the period to replace Reason in its relationship with Faith and Revelation. With this qualitative change the "will" of the individual personality was transformed into interconnected levels of ecstatic state to register the view available at various gradations of the total reality. In retrospect, however, it was the creative experience which laid the foundation of mystic poetry in the Islamic world and was recognised as the basic principle of gnosis. The life of feeling became the central area of affirmation of faith and the available framework of logical construction and theological positivism was extended to include justification of faith in terms of the data supplied by creative experience. In its application to practical behaviour, the life of feeling permeated the language of love and was, in this way, capable of guiding the fragmented human psyche towards its desired object.

Hallaj's *ana al-haqq* belonged to the perspective briefly outlined above. It was, indeed, the historic demand of the thought-currents of the period which impelled Hallaj to establish an immediate relationship between faith and revelation.

(3)

However, *ana al-haqq* as it stands has raised a few literary questions as well and, within the tradition of mystic poetry, the attitude preserved in Hallaj's expression has given rise to mixed reactions regarding its content. It is held that it is an exaggeration of subjective experience, and *ana*—the personal "I"—shows leanings towards megalomania and egotism. It is the personal "I" which overshadows *al-haqq*, and thereby invites total attention to itself. In fact, the personal "I" absorbs *al-haqq*, and reaches out to the romantic cult of the egotistical sublime. In this context the truth tends to become subjective and, therefore, relative, and in its social implications it shows the possibility of numerous diversions. Extreme individualism, in contrast to institutionalism, is also held to be related to *ana al-haqq*. The personal "I" is supposed to be potentionally explosive and destructive for values of the Establishment. A.J. Arberry has summed up the position by saying that Hallaj had dared to declare that his direct awareness of God was for him a clearer proof than both revelation and reason.

The personal "I," however, in Hallaj's verses does not possess an identity of its own; it is in a state of perpetual transformation. It is a movement between fast changing conditions of experience. Its identity is established only in reference to the third-person pronoun: he, and to its objective form: him. In fact, this pronoun (he/him) activates the personal "I" and becomes its destiny within the spectrum of experience. *Ana*, as will, ceases to exist by itself, and instead the distant "will" of the other pronoun operates on it as an overpowering will. In the process the personal "I" surrenders itself to the gravitation of an all-embracing experience, and the I-Thou relationship appears in place of the distant third- and first-person relationship of "He" and "I". At all stages of inner movement within the poetry of Hallaj's verse the personal "I" remains without identity and whatever being it seems to possess is bestowed upon it by the emerging relationship. "He" and "Thou" determine the personal "I" and its identity depends upon that determination. The cult of egotistical sublime is hardly supported by the textual study of Hallaj's verse.

The intimate experience contained in the poetry of Hallaj's verse is an important evidence to show that the personal "I" does not incline towards unification within I-Thou or He-I relationship, as the three entities move at different planes of reality. As for *ana* being without identity, its individuation is sustained throughout this relationship. And in between *al-haqq* and *ana* only an objective and emotionally charged entity—represented by "He" and "Thou"—appears to cover the entire poetic landscape. This formulates a new equation between *ana*, the entity He-Thou and *al-haqq*. Thus *ana al-haqq* as a statement of experience retains He-Thou as point of reference within itself. The history of mystic poetry has throughout supported this point of reference and transference of meaning in mystic poetry has been achieved only through this reference.

(4)

Ana al-haqq has been treated so far in the context of the Sufic tradition. It has, throughout the tradition, maintained a theoretical position which was simultaneously corroborated by Hallaj's biography. But somehow the phrase could not draw its objective valuation from its textual background preserved in Hallaj's notable work : *Tawasin. Ana al-haqq* has so deeply rooted itself in its timeless setting that its existence in time, in a real work by Hallaj, has been almost omitted by scholars of Islamic mysticism. It seems appropriate, therefore, to place *ana al-haqq* within the thought-pattern of *Tawasin*, and to determine its significance with reference to the text of *Tawasin*.

Tawasin is a collection of ten books dealing with questions raised by the Science of Divine Unity. "Book Eleven – The Garden of Gnosis," which is the last book in *Kitab al-Tawasin*, edited by Massignon, is a critique of the philosophic position of the Divine Unity. The attitude throughout *Tawasin* is intellectually objective and the approach towards questions is almost analytical. There are indications of sound logical training also. The language carries the imprint of a mind which is educated in the methodology of reasoning proper to the Science of Divine Unity. It is, therefore, relatively colourless, though at certain levels of argument it tends to become figurative. However, two different planes are very obvious in the language when the reasoning is imperceptibly absorbed by extracts from the Quranic Text. The language is thus repeatedly strengthened and interpreted by the Quranic text. In this manner, the thought-process is nourished and matured by the sacred reference. Taken on its totality the language of *Tawasin* exists as an objective correlative of the kind of experience which informs and shapes its author's biography. *Tawasin* is the spiritual life-story of Hallaj. As such it can amply help in establishing thc textual context and the meaning of *ana al-haqq*.

Since *al-haqq* has been traditionally interpreted as theosophic equivalent of God, it will be proper to make an approach to it in the light of the last book of *Tawasin,* namely, "The Garden of Gnosis"—which discusses the doctrine of Divine Unity.

Unknowability of the Divine Essence, says Hallaj, is the basic principle of all human activity as the Divine Essence is beyond the categories of intellectual knowledge. The contingent world, the finitude of sense-data, the logical construction of reason or the relational mode of analogy are hardly the required apparatus for any understanding of the Oneness which lies beyond all comprehension. In fact, the mind brought up and trained in the dimensions of time and space cannot move out of the created world and reach the unknowable Divine Essence. Through the being or the annihilation of the self, or by the attributes or the limit-situation of human helplessness, or with reference to the idea of the two extremes of individual life and death, the human comprehension cannot approach the Essence. In fact, His manifestation in the phenomena, the logical construction to prove Him, the idea of the Infinite, or just pure ignorance are veils covering the Secret of the One Who is eternal in His Oneness. It is impossible to name Him either, because to name and be named contradict the essential oneness of the Divine Being. What the human mind can at least know through its finite activity, cognitive act or experiential data is the state of alienation of the creation from its Creator. A gulf is simply fixed between the infinite and the finitude. Towards the end of the Book ("Garden of Gnosis"), Hallaj exclaims :

"The True remains the True, the Creator as Creator and

what belongs to things created remains as things created. This always is . . ." (*Bustan* : 26).

However, *ana* as an extension of the human condition, and as an inseparable part of the created things, assumes the role of attestation in terms of awe and self-alienation, and also of awareness that it is surrounded by an eternal Divine Presence. *Ana* perpetually lives within the environment of *al-haqq*. It will also be obvious that *ana* and *al-haqq*, by virtue of the theosophic position, cannot enter into a unitive state; the two remain eternally separate and the gulf between them remains unbridged. The mystic phrase splits into its components and *ana* is placed in a theosophic setting where *al-haqq* is unknowable and unproven. *Tasin* 10 reinforces the same argument by observing that the attempt to prove the Divine Being converts God into a created god (*Tasin* 10 : 11 and 13).

(5)

Thus viewing *ana al-haqq* in its separateness, it would seem plausible that in its biographical context the expression has a spoken and not a written relevance. In fact, it is the Voice, the human voice, which vitalises it, and not the compactness of its word arrangement as it has been traditionally held. The voice operates at the first component (*ana*) and activates it and then, with some pause, operates at the other (*al-haqq*). The personal "I" calls for the Truth, for the One, in its Oneness, for God—as if in the wilderness of unknowability.

The phonal activity thus becomes a warning, a reminder —and almost a cry of the alienated human spirit for the unknowable Creator. This phonal activity has succeeded in contributing the doctrine of Reunion to Islamic mystic poetry.

(6)

The experience of Divine unknowability does not emerge as a negative experience. In fact, it affirms the theological position of an unseen God and confirms the truth of this belief. However, the unknowability of the Divine Being transforms the created universe and its time-scale into a moment in eternity, and the unknowable becomes an eternal presence. This in its turn refers to the wonder of created objects and to a universe which does not lie within the measurement of human time-scale, and offers a physico-theological framework to make any movement possible in the direction of the Supreme Being (*Tasin* 5 : 13-15). Thus, movement from one form of greatness to another annihilates the human condition to such a degree that the Supreme and the unconditioned Being alone appears as the Real and the True (*Tasin* 2 : 3-4; 10: 23). In this context the personal "I," *ana*, disintegrates to confirm the Supreme Presence of God.

The personal "I," which is eternally placed in the presence of God, is in fact surrounded by the circles of Divine attributes. It is through the working of the Divine Will that the personal "I" is made aware of the

Divine Presence. The will makes it a felt presence (*Tasin* 7 : 1 and 5). The Divine Will leads to Divine Wisdom, Divine Power and Divine Knowledge, and then to His Eternality and Ever-livingness. These six attributes enable the personal "I" to be aware of the Divine Presence. The awareness possessed by *ana* is, therefore, attributive. In this manner the Divine Presence becomes a felt and living presence. The personal "I" can approach God only through and with the help of the idea of Divine Presence which in its turn is made actual by attributes. This is the only way of human knowledge and it is only through it that man can receive God, and his own life of feeling is enriched by Divine Presence. But these principal attributes are the realisation of theosophic perception, and the Divine Presence still very much remains an unrealised experience. Hallaj points out Divine Compassion as another attribute which makes it possible for the personal "I," *ana*, to enter into a silent and contemplative dialogue with God (*Tasin* 10 : 24). The unknowability of God is received as Divine Compassion by man. The human cry of isolation is answered by compassion. But the ascending path leading to Divine Compassion begins with man's unconditional yes to the Divine Will.

(7)

As attributive totality, Divine Compassion has entered human history as Revelation and as the luminous form of the Prophet of Islam. The light coming from the Luminous Form is the Revelation which affirms Divine Compassion, and through it the totality of attributes and the all-embracing Divine Presence. Theosophically, a new relationship is established between Revelation, Luminous Form of the Holy Prophet and Divine Presence (*Tasin* 1 : 1-16). The Revelation has not only affirmed the Divine Presence, it has also confirmed the existence of God through the texture of the Quranic language. In *Tasin* 6, Hallaj says :

> "And there is none to have
> said He is : The One,
> except Ahmad, and peace be upon
> him, and to him alone has He
> appeared in Vision within
> Vision."

In Hallajian theosophic framework the attestation of the existence of God is directly related to the light of the Prophet Muhammad. Only in his prophetic state has the Divine Being entered the area of contemplation and His reported existence has become actual existence. The transmitted fact has become the felt experience in the Ascension of the Holy Prophet. The transmitted fact is thus attested by the felt experience. In this context the Revelation and the Ascension give evidence of the Divine Being in terms of felt experience (*Tasin* 2 : 3-4).

Elaborating the prophetic state in the theosophic framework Hallaj further says (*Tasin* 1 : 11) :

> "Truth is with him, and what is measured
> and what is unmeasured is also with him.
> In Presence he is the first and he is

> the last in the line of messengers;
> he is the hidden meaning of
> Creation, and the
> manifest meaning of the knowledge
> of the Essence. . . ."

Thus, truth is located and, as such, existentiated in the being of the "Luminous Form" of the Prophet Muhammad. Truth is inseparable from the luminosity of the prophetic mission. Hallaj is fully convinced of this theosophic position which is made even more explicit in the following (*Tasin* 1 : 17):

> "If you leave and escape to lands away
> from him you will find no way, and none
> to own you.
> O sick in soul, you will see no one to
> save you. The Wise talk of the Wisest of
> the World is like sandhills before him."

In the same *Tasin* (1 : 14) Hallaj further observes:

> "And the truth has not led him
> to created things for who He is,
> He is : and where He is, and where
> and who and what He is—He is,
> He is, He is. . . ."

The theosophic framework is orientated towards the luminous form of the Holy Prophet and the truth is implicitly defined as the relationship between Revelation and the manifest God in the Revelation; the luminous form is established as the attestation and transmission of the Truth. The Luminous Form, in fact, covers the entire theosophic background of *Tawasin* and the questions relevant to the science of Divine Unity are answered in reference to the Luminous Form. The

Truth is authenticated in the Holy Prophet. Referring to this, as the total Truth, Hallaj says (*Tasin* 1 : 15):

> "And none who knows or who knows
> he knows has ever gone beyond the
> 'mim' of Muhammad ; there is no way out
> for him ; likewise
> who ever moves within has never gone beyond
> the 'hay' of Muhammad ; the 'hay' leads to
> the second 'mim' and the letter
> 'dal' brings back to the first 'mim'."

Explaining the underlying suggestions of the alphabetic letters, Hallaj says that the last letter "dal" (د) in the name of the Holy Prophet stands for the ever-present essence of the Prophetic Revelation, the "mim" (م) stands for the relational position in truth, the "hay" (ح) represents the inner state of being, which itself meets the extension in time in the second "mim" (م) of the Holy Prophet's name. In this context the Truth, the Revelation and the Luminous Form appear as the unitive act of the unseen God.

(8)

Hallaj has laid special emphasis on the epistemological significance of the attributes. The attributes are the only discoverable limits of the human knowledge. In *Tasin* 10 : 18, Hallaj has made the observation that the knowledge of the Divine Being is impossible without the knowledge of the attributes. Only the attributes can be comprehended by man. Thus, three separate dimensions are presented to understanding, namely, (1) the unknowability of God and the human reason, (2) the knowledge of attributes in their totality and the doctrine of Divine Presence, and (3) the Revelation and the Idea of the Luminous Form. In *Tawasin*, (1) is made to support (2) and the position thus made available is accepted for the attestation of (3). Except for (3) there is no other way of knowing God or to have any idea of His existence. The Revelation has vindicated the existence of God ; and the light of the Luminous Form of Muhammad is enough and the most reliable to discover the Truth. The knowledge of the existence of God is the only and the ultimate Truth. *Al-haqq* of Hallaj refers to that Truth.

(9)

In the studies of Hallaj much attention has been given to the personal "I," and the *ana* in the mystic phrase *ana al-haqq* has been variously interpreted. But the personal "I" has probably been studied against some vague background of sufic thought, which has aroused mixed feelings in the tradition of Islamic mysticism. In fact, the personal "I," *ana*, stands within the perspective outlined above. Textually too, *ana* does not have any reference without the dimensions and the perspectives which are available in *Tawasin*. In *Tasin* 2, while observing the relation between the received fact and the felt experience (*Tasin* 2 : 2-4) Hallaj says :

"But he who is given to instincts

> and their desires, and who is
> weak in thought and who wears sin as
> dress for mortal life, will never meet
> success, like me."
>
> "O if you think that I am
> One who has reached that state or
> who will ever reach that state,
> Or had reached that state sometime
> in the past, O ! never, never, never !
> I am on my way to His discovery, on my
> way that leads to Him. O ! I belong to
> Him, and He does not own me yet" (*Tasin* 2 : 5-6).

In *Tasin* 6:25 the same strain of feeling is more pronounced when he says :

> "If I be killed or put alive on gibbet,
> or my hands and feet cut off,
> even then I will never go back
> on my word."

In these extracts the personal "I," *ana*, assumes its relevance in terms of the He-Thou relationship which has already been considered. It has also an inner basic sense of commitment which is meaningful only in terms of that relationship. However, within the perspective already suggested the He-Thou relationship becomes significant only when it is placed within the framework of Revelation and its truth. Hallaj's commitment holds steadfastly only to that truth which is manifest in Revelation and has become accessible through the doctrine of the Luminous Form. The personal "I," as it appears in *Tawasin*, exists to justify the values of faith in the wilderness of Divine unknowability.

(10)

Haqq (Truth) and *Haqiqah* (Reality) appear as two different and independent concepts in *Tawasin.* They are invested with distinct connotations and at no point in *Tawasin* the terms are held to be interchangeable. The Truth is beyond Reality, though in their mutual relationship Reality is at a lower level of cognition than Truth. In *Tasin* 2, Hallaj says :

> "Truth is beyond Reality—as something unidentified and Reality is apart from Truth. . . ."

Illustrating the position figuratively, Hallaj observes (*Tasin* 2 : 2-3) :

> "The light shed by Flame is the Knowledge of Reality and its Warmth suggests The Real that lies within that knowledge ; but to enter its Warmth and to know its light thereby is Truth."

In *Tasin* 3 : 8, Reality is further explained byH allaj in its relationship with the created objects :

> "Thus Reality remains reality and the created things as things created ; O ! leave and pass beyond the things created that you become Reality itself."

Reality is also that point of cognition were the contingent and the finite dissolve and cease to be objective entities. This is elaborated in *Tasin* 5 : 32 :

> "Then, what is Reality ? A point where the links with World contingent exist no more, its pains, and pangs and

So now come back
no more."

Thus Reality is a dimension of the contingent and the finite. It is a collection of sense-data. But notwithstanding its origin, it exists as an abstraction on the outer limits of the contingent and the finite. In this sense Reality is a construction deduced from the sense-data of the contingent world. Reality is the realm of reason, and as such it is possible to mark all those various stages within it which affect the horizontal movement of man (*Tasin* 3:1). Reality gives the geometry of being only. It is in this context that it has appeared in various books of *Tawasin*.

(11)

Nicholson has rendered *haqiqah* as Truth in his translation of the account about Sahl al-Tustari in *Kashf al-Mahjub*, but he has also rendered into English the Hallajian term of *al-haqq* as the Truth. Thus, Truth in his rendering has a vagueness about it as it is used as an interchangeable term both for *haqq* and *haqiqah*. In fact, there is a sharp difference in meaning between the two terms and the text of *Tawasin* supports the viewpoint. If, however, in al-Tustari's sufic thought the concept of Truth contained within it the dimensions of *haqiqah*, the conclusion can conveniently be drawn that there exists a fundamental difference in approach between al-Tustari and Hallaj in their conceptual view of Truth. Commenting on what is meant by Truth (*haqiqah*), Ali Hujwiri points out that Truth as *haqiqah* is inseparably connected with Law (*Shari'ah*) and that the Law is the Truth and the Truth is the Law. The rejection of the Truth, according to him, is infidelity and polytheism. This latter statement gives a negative definition to Truth. Positively, however, the Truth is defined as the creed of Muslim faith; there is no god save Allah, is the Truth. The Truth, in fact, is the knowledge of God.

Thus, *haqiqah* as Truth was an exoteric concept in the days of Hallaj, though it had later on assumed depth and extension in meaning by the time of the writing of *Kashf al-Mahjub*. In the formative years of Hallaj's career as a theosophic thinker, the influence of Sahl al-Tustari, who was his teacher at Tustar, can hardly be overlooked. Al-Tustari did not hold the Law and the Truth as separate entities and had suggested that the Law itself could not integrate the human personality. Therefore, its combination with *haqiqah* (the Truth) was an indispensable requirement of the Muslim thought. Al-Tustari's emphasis on the integration of the two had in fact laid stress on *haqiqah* in the scale of religious values. This made the Truth, at least in its exoteric aspect, the major issue of the age.

Truth had also become an object of search for mystics in the contemporary intellectual milieu of Hallaj. Abu Uthman al-Hiri has observed that in his childhood he was continually seeking the Truth, and the externalists (the Scholars of the Law) inspired him with a feeling of abhorrence. He has informed that he perceived that the sacred Law concealed a mystery under the superficial forms which are (in general) followed by the majority of the believers. In later years, however, he met Yahya b. Mu'adh and found there the mystery that, he said, was the object of his search. The mystery that al-Hiri discovered in the company of Yahya b. Mu'adh was the idea of devotion to God based on the emotions of fear and hope; the devotion for God was the total absorption in the contemplation of God. The mystery rested in enabling man to have direct and immediate knowledge of God. This made it possible for man, in search of Truth, to move from the word to its meaning, and from its meaning to the true information about Him derived from sight as was taught by Junaid in his circle. The Truth consisted in transformation of reported and transmitted information into felt experience.

Love and ecstasy entered the outlines of Truth with al-Khawwas and 'Uthman al-Makki, and the contemplation of God in terms of devotion became a state which was beyond all explanation. It was indeed this point of awareness which was the object of the mystic search for Truth. With this development in Muslim creative thought the Reality as *haqiqah* became the Truth as *al-haqq*. *Haqiqah* as formal exoteric reality permeated the psychic structure and re-emerged as *al-haqq*.

(12)

It might, however, be said, figuratively, that the Truth (*al-haqq*) was flowering of the Reality (*haqiqah*) which was nourished by the Muslim creative thought during the period which was contemporary with Hallaj. But, like all flowering, it was sweet and regenerating though vague and beyond concrete reference. The Truth had the philosophic notion of the Divine (God) as its subject of knowledge and all effort in this direction produced physico-theological awareness accompanied by the feelings of awe for the Creator as the First Cause or the Cosmic Being. At best, the plurality dissolved into the Unity, and al-Nuri could say that Union with God is separation from all else, and separation from all else is Union with Him. The experience was collected and interpreted to affirm the theological position, in other words, the data drawn from the search for Truth were used to enrich the content of the sacred Law and the Community.

Junaid's assertion that true information is derived from sight, but what forms the central principle of Hallaj's thought in *Tawasin* could not agree to the subjective definition of the Truth. God could neither be contained in subjective definitions nor could He be approached with the logical apparatus of the mind. This was indeed an acute crisis in the life of contemporary thought and much depended on how the crisis was to be resolved by the thinkers of the age. The unknowability of God in the available logical terms had made God inaccessible, and as a corollary to it the world and the phenomena became mechanistic, and human situation came under the rule of indifferent and callous Fate. The temporal history of the age is simply an extension of this development in thought. On the other hand, the subjective approach to God created either a body of self-absorbed experience or simple reliance on dream psychology. The subjective approach had an important advantage however, as it signalled the deep-lying quest for God and necessitated the resolution of the crisis in regard to the identity of the Truth.

(13)

Truth, in *Tawasin*, draws its content from the historic phenomenon of revelation. In *Tasin* 1, the Truth appears within the following perspective; the extract given below occurs in the opening paragraph of *Tawasin* :

> "Thus he [Hallaj] said (may Allah be pleased with him)
> *Tasin* . . .
> it was a shining form of light from the
> Unseen, and it appeared and illumined,
> and returned to the Unseen, and it
> surpassed all lights and became the
> light of lights, and its brightness spread
> across all the moons. Its
> luminous apex has gone up beyond the
> skies which are
> surrounded by mystery."

This theosophy of light, which is followed later by reference to Truth, is principally dependent on the Quranic attestation that Allah is the light of the heavens and of the earth. However, the light is referred to the

Unseen which is the Unknowable of the human reason. The light flashes in a moment of time; it appears, illumines and returns to the Unseen, but in the duration when it instantaneously enters the phenomenal reality, it overpowers the vertical dimensions of knowledge. Thus where? why? and how? are silenced before its mystery. The Unseen and its manifestation of light remain a mystery; the *Tawasin* discloses its meaning against this background and within this perspective. Truth is situated in the perspective supplied by the Unseen and its theosophy of light. The extract given above may be read in continuation with the following:

> "Truth (*Haqq*) named him *Ummi*
> to assure him; called him One
> of the Sacred House to regard him
> in his greatness; and named him
> Makki for his fixed and unchanging
> station and for the nearness that
> he had with
> Truth (*Haqq*) itself."

These lines would point out that Truth as a notion is in its active nature related to the Unseen only through the medium of the light; it is not the Unseen or the Unknowable. Truth is the manifestation of light as it is received by the Configurative Object (represented by the titles of *Taha*, *Yasin* and *al-Nur*) who is none other than Muhammad, the messenger of Allah. Truth is, therefore, the revealed light, the unique phenomenon of revelation; in fact, the Quran in its mystery of the Revelation.

However, when Truth (*Haqq*) is placed in relationship with the created objects, its meaning can be derived from the Divine imperative to be, and from the existence of the created objects. Thus, Truth stands for the transcendental creative urge; and even in this context it (Truth) remains the manifestation and the interpreter of light. In this sense the created objects become the signs of the revealed light and Truth interprets them in the language of the light. Hallaj considers the Truth as revelation (*Tasin* 3:10) and the Revelation as Light (*Tasin* 5:20) and fully attests that the Truth is with the Messenger of Allah (*Tasin* 1:11). In *Tasin* 1:5 Truth (*Haqq*) is also described as the principle of rediscovery of the value of faith. Truth, in this framework, suggests a plane of knowledge which is beyond the reach of intellectual reasoning (*Tasin* 1:9). It is one, unique and indivisible, and is never subject to change (*Tasin* 8:1, 10:6). The Truth, Hallaj affirms, became word on the Prophet's voice (*Tasin* 1:9).

Thus, the Truth in Hallajian metaphysics shows deviation from the conventional attributive meaning and its synonymous equation with God. It is the light from the Unseen entering the phenomenal reality which is the Truth, and which discovers its expression in the Prophetic Being. The Luminous Form of Muhammad is the Prophetic Being illumined by the Truth and its light. The Ascension of the Prophet offers attestation of the Divine Being Whose attributive totality appears as revelation and becomes the Truth when the same is received by the Prophet. The Revelation confirms the belief in the Unseen God.

(14)

In the *Tawasin*, Hallaj makes a clear distinction in meaning between *Haqq* (Truth) and *al-Haqq* (the Truth), and accordingly it becomes obvious that the two concepts are hardly interchangeable. "Truth" as general and theosophic notion suggests the Revelation in terms of Faith, and as such it is beyond the dimensions of phenomenal reality. But it is simultaneously existent in time as an event in history. In this perspective *Haqq* (Truth/Revelation) connects the historical with the eternal, and its existence as Word of God is an open evidence of His presence. Hallaj uses *al-haqq* in a specific and well-defined sense in *Tasin* 9 : 6 as follows :

> "*Al-haqq* is the place of return for
> *Haqq*, and in no way
> *Haqq*
> itself. . . ."

The distinction between the two suggests a perpetual transaction, a movement between them. *Al-haqq* is the point in space and time to which *Haqq* in its own way and according to its own providential scheme returns. *Al-haqq* becomes the Truth only when it is visited by *Haqq*, and in the absence of *Haqq*, *al-haqq* loses its identity; it ceases to be. The existence of *al-haqq* is dependent upon its contact with Truth. Any milieu unvisited by *Haqq* is a condemned and contingent milieu where the human ego is shattered in instinctive anarchy.

In the tradition of Sufism, the notion : *al-haqq* has

been used to represent the attributive aspect of the Divine, and has been popularly understood to mean God. But this attributive designation seems a post-Hallajian development as the standardisation of sufic vocabulary was not wholly accomplished by the time of Hallaj. Besides, apart from the status of a Divine attribute, *al-haqq* had its own philosophical and semantic ramifications. It had its definite place in the development of thought, and it also exercised influence as final verdict in dubious moral or intellectual situations. Hallaj's distinction between *Haqq* and *al-haqq* would have certainly lost its seriousness if the two had meant one and the same notion, or if *al-haqq* had been assigned the status of the Unseen or of the Unknowable. *Al-haqq* could not even become the One, and consequently remain inaccessible to Knowledge. However, if *al-haqq* were at all given the value of the Unknowable, then the knowledge of the Truth remained for ever a closed book to mankind. This was obviously against the spirit of inquiry available in the age of Hallaj.

Al-haqq, however, draws its significance from the relativity of truths which was the outcome of theological and philosophical disputation. The Truth can emerge only in a milieu of conflicting truths. In isolation, or against a scheme of timelessness, the Truth (*al-haqq*) cannot have an objective correlative as it inclines towards unknowability in such perspective. At best, *al-haqq* can exist only as an abstraction and that too within human surroundings ; it is a personified abstraction. *Haqq* (Truth), as defined earlier, extends allegorical personification to *al-Haqq* (the Truth).

(15)

The view given above suggests reversal of the perspective in which *al-haqq* has been traditionally placed both as notion and object. Thus, with Hallaj, a distinctive dimension of thought had emerged in which the personal "I" had acquired the central position, and the questions relating to Divine Unity were to be treated in terms of data available from the central position. It was a strange phenomenon as it gave a human framework to a theological and doctrinal notion. It was in this context, therefore, that *Haqq* (Truth) was seen to be the manifestation of Light in the Revelation, and in the idea of the Luminous Form, and that *al-Haqq* (the Truth) became as allegorical personification of *Haqq* itself. This perspective established a new but fundamental relationship between *al-haqq*, the Luminous Form and Truth (*Haqq*) as manifestation of Light from the Unseen. In the history of Islamic mystic poetry this relationship became the essential content of the He-Thou relationship.

Al-haqq as an initial stage, within this perspective, existed as an abstraction which assumed a concrete location in time and place only through the medium of personal "I" (*ana*) to become a personified abstraction to win the primary affections of human milieu towards the Luminous Form of Muhammad, and to observe thereby the manifested light in the Revelation which for ever attests the attributive totality and compassion of the Unseen God. The absorption of *al-haqq* within the psychological structure of the personal "I," *ana*, vindicated the objective truth of the Prophecy and the ontological manifestation of the Unseen in the Revelation. Thus total man, and not an exclusive faculty, became the universal witness of the Divine mystery. *Al-haqq* looked at the Unseen through the intermediary assistance of the Luminous Form only and without this mediation *al-haqq*, both as personification and abstraction, could not have any claim to existence. *Al-haqq* existed by Muhammad and in Muhammad only. In Hallajian metaphysics, *ana*, the personal "I," remains for ever in quest of *al-haqq* to know the Beloved Messenger of Allah and through his benign eyes reach out to the mystery made explicit in the Revelation.

(16)

Ana al-haqq as the definite expression occurs in *Tasin* 6:23 where the question of confusion concerning eternal Scheme of Existence is discussed in a dramaturgic presentation. *Tasin* 6 is itself placed almost in the middle of *Tawasin*, and as such it is supported by the thought-patterns of the books preceding and following it. The intellectual vision which emerges in *Tawasin*, therefore, gives a richer context to *Tasin* 6, which continues the thought-process and at the same time affirms its content. The dramaturgic presentation places Iblis, the devil and Satan of popular thought, in its timeless setting, and Pharaoh, the Sun-King of the ancient Nile valley, in the background of serial time, and offers an explication of the Divine Will within this clearly defined framework. Iblis and Pharaoh interpret and define their respective positions, first in terms of predetermined act, and secondly in terms of limitations placed on their individual acts by the compulsion of the predetermined will. They justify their state, and in that justification discover their own principle of obedience, though in this respect the positions upheld by Iblis and Pharaoh differ considerably from each other. The two, in consequence, cause inversion of the value of obedience, and succeed as archetypal characters, in introducing confusion in the eternal scheme of existence.

In *Tasin* 6, Iblis is presented in the very beginning as the figure which has been irretrievably confined within the Being itself. The notion of the Being appears as a very powerful passion in Iblis' pattern of thinking. He is immovably concerned with the Divine Unity, and fails to show any awareness of other Divine attributes. His approach is almost mathematical, and his reasoning as to Divine Unity hardly displays any sign of belief in the manifestation of the Divine Will in the phenomenon and particularly in the creation of man. The creation ceases to be an evidence of the Divine attributes for him. Consequently, Iblis' thought-process works from abstraction to abstraction without any reference to observation or sense-data derived from sight. His rigorous attitude only enables him to worship the

Creator as Pure Abstraction. However, beyond the state of pure abstraction Iblis could approach only the state of estrangement, and when he reached there he could not but emerge as one "who is unreliable and therefore shaken in thought". In *Tasin* 6 it is at this stage that Iblis is commanded to pay homage to Adam, and thereby affirm obedience to the Divine Will. Iblis, in his turn, refuses to carry out the command and offers a persuasive justification of his act. He says :

> "My deflection is the outcome of Your
> Transcendence, of Your purity ; and
> my reason is my madness for You. I
> know none but You, and Adam is none but
> other than You. In between You and I, there
> none exists ; if aught exists, it is
> I" (*Tasin* 6 : 10).

Iblis' concern with the Divine Being transmutes into concern with his own self. The Being is, in deflection, replaced by his own being. Continuing the justification, Iblis further says :

> "For me there is no way to what is
> other than You ; and I am of their side
> who side with reason, and who go for
> reason . . . and it was none else
> but me who knew You in pre-existence,
> in time before time. In preference
> I come before anyone else as I stayed perpetually
> in obedience before any of Your creation
> did ever know obedience. Thus Your knowing is
> mine, and in inclination, You lean
> towards me and I do lean towards You. And this
> our leaning between us is far far ancient
> than ancient time itself. So why should I

prostrate before one who is not You but
other than You. And so deflection ; there was
no choice, no way, no other
act left but what I did. The fire which gave
me form attracts me back to
fire. And fire begets fire. The will is
Yours ; and whatever You now
determine is, as ever
Yours.
In separation from You there is no other aloofness
left for me ; and I realise that far and near
are simple words
without content ; for I have gone so far and
away from You. And I have made
separation from You
my friend—companion in my plight.
And who could name it such,
though love it be, and just appear
estrangement from You" (*Tasin* 6 : 11-12).

In the context of above citations it will be obvious that Iblis mainly represents a state of mind which is governed by his passion for reason (intellect/*al-'aql*). His idea of obedience is also conditioned by that state of mind. There seems to be no other dimension present in his thought-structure. He credits himself with the honour to be the first among the elemental forms who had the earliest success in knowing the Creator and also in identifying the knowledge of His Being. This knowledge, however, bears marks of high intellection and develops a faith in the uncompromising Oneness of the Divine Being. The mutual leaning between the Creator and the protagonist (Iblis) displays underlying suggestions to al-Kindi (d. 873) and to his definition of Agent

Intellect (*'aql fa''al*) which "proceeds from God by way of emanation and which, though acting on the faculties of the body, is independent of body, as its knowledge is not based upon perceptions obtained through the senses". It is through the mediation of al-Kindi's Agent Intellect that the "mutual leaning" as emphasised by Iblis has become possible between God and His uncompromising creation, Iblis.

In the dramaturgic presentation Iblis is a personified abstraction and as such he stands outside the world-tradition of the Devil in its multiple forms. The character portrayal of Satan in the old English *Fall of the Angels*, which is almost contemporary with the age of Hallaj, possesses humanity which is almost non-existent in Iblis of Hallajian metaphysics. Iblis has nothing human in him as he is a pure abstraction, and as such the state of mind it represents tends to become a structure of abstract thought. His structural condition isolates him in the eternal scheme of existence and is responsible for his aloofness from God. In the dramaturgic presentation Iblis is not the traditional Satan of the popular belief; he is the archetypal character in which the Mind has withdrawn itself from the data supplied by the senses. This inner condition repels him from entering into any understanding with Adam who represents the total human personality, and also compels him (Iblis) to retain the supremacy of the intellect over the other subordinate faculties of the human soul. Iblis' arrogance is, therefore, the outcome of the latent complusions in the structure of his thought.

In his origin from fire, Iblis reveals and equally

important aspect of his archetypal character. The fire does not suggest the presence of light and becomes even more suggestive by the omission. The Hallajian metaphysics is basically a theosophy of light; in the form of the flame, the heat emitted is just the peripheral reality and not the self-luminous truth. In his origin, therefore, Iblis approaches the peripheral reality, and his mode of knowledge, in the absence of light, becomes total blindness recklessly motivated by an intense passion for reason. Hallaj's emphasis on sight and observation explains the incompleteness of Iblis' knowledge of Divine Unity. Iblis' blindness causes confusion in the eternal scheme of existence.

Iblis' assertion on "mutual leaning" between him and God, which also suggests the emanation of Agent Intellect, raises a metaphysical question. How is it that Iblis fails to truly recognise the Divine Will underlying the commandment of God in the given situations? Is it that Agent Intellect is purely a knowing faculty and not a discriminating faculty? And that Iblis lacks that discriminating faculty because of his origin, and, therefore, fails to act in the light of Divine Wisdom. In fact, the "Intellect" referred to by Iblis does not have any corresponding potential faculty within him, and therefore Agent Intellect does not awaken any potential faculty in Iblis and arouse it to activity as it does in man according to Farabi's (d. 950) viewpoint. Technically, there is no response to the Divine commandment in Iblis except the vigorous insistence on awareness of the Divine Unity. In Iblis, the intellect is isolated to assess and examine its reactions to the Divine Will.

Tasin 7 gives a fuller view of Iblis' state of mind and points out Iblis' total isolation from the primary Divine attributes of Will, Wisdom, Power, Knowledge and Eternity. In the eternal scheme of existence Iblis appears at a much lower level of possibility than man (Adam).

(17)

The dramaturgic presentation, by implication, suggests Man to be superior to Iblis in terms of possibilities within the framework of the primary Divine attributes. But Man (Adam) in the eternal setting appears only as pure possibility. However, when he appears in historical time, the possibility is tried in another archetypal character, Pharaoh, the Sun-King of ancient Nile valley. In *Tasin* 6 : 22, the Pharaoh is presented to describe his situation as under:

> "And Pharaoh said : I know not that
> you have any god but me ;
> And he had known no one
> among his people to discriminate,
> to choose between the truth
> and the un-truth, between the True
> and the false."

The Pharaoh is far more submissive than Iblis for compulsions of the human condition. Nevertheless, his situation is the outcome of alienation from any knowledge of God. The intellectual structure which informs Iblis is virtually inoperative in the character of the Sun-King. He is also without any contact with the discriminating intelligence. The reason has failed him externally as Agent Intellect and internally as potential intelligence. Therefore, his knowledge is confined to finitude, and he defines himself in terms of the Creator. In Hallajian metaphysics, the human condition, which deteriorates to such an indiscriminate level, stands in utter need of Prophecy because it is only through its mediation that man can re-establish his contact with the Manifest Light. However, in *Tasin* 6 : 24, this human archetypal character, the Pharaoh, reclaims his latent possibility when he is confronted with limit-situation.

These two archetypal characters present a state of alienation in the eternal scheme of existence; Iblis represents the alienated intellect, while the Pharaoh represents the state of alienation of the human condition. In fact, the state of alienation has discovered its archetypal expression in the characters drawn from religious sources. One thing, however, which deserves special mention, is the character of Iblis which is essentially a secular representation. Iblis does not seem to have any resemblance with Satan of the *Book of Genesis*; he is also superficially identical with the Fallen Angel of the Muslim religious tradition. The best approach to *Tawasin's* Iblis can probably be found in Milton's *Paradise Lost*. The intellectual sophistry of Iblis in *Tawasin* is similar to the sophistry of Milton's Satan in the Temptation episode of *Paradise Lost*. The same holds equally true in the characterisation of Pharaoh, who, while representing the alienated human condition, draws his significance from the limit-situation of the agony of death. The limit-situation wins him over from alienation to re-education, and he saves himself from his own hollow vision of self-deification. Behind these archetypal characters it is rather easy to feel the rhythm of the contemporary climate of ideas of the age of Hallaj; the alienated intellect and the alienated human condition collectively represent the intellectual and social milieu of the Hallajian world.

(18)

The Hallajian position with reference to these archetypal characters (Iblis and Pharaoh) stands in need of clarification as some of Hallaj scholars are of the view that Hallaj is sympathetically inclined towards them, and that he considers them as his mentors and guides in strict contravention of Muslim religious opinion. Most Hallaj scholars consider Iblis and Pharaoh as cosmic and historical characters and place them in a negative perspective within the popular religious valuation. Hallaj, indeed, considers these characters as negative forces, but there is hardly any indication in *Tawasin* that he accords them any preferential status at all. In *Tasin* 6 : 18-19, Hallaj's views about the Fallen Angel are noteworthy. He says:

> "Many are the views about Azazil;
> he is the one who warns in the heaven
> and on the earth; on the sky
> he bade the angels see whatever be
> good, and on the earth he bade
> man see the evil; and good is
> known by its opposite and evil is

known by what contradicts it.
The fine silken cloth is made by the
Coarse thread taken from rude and
coarse cloth. In the same manner
the King brings forth the things good
and the things evil, and suggests
choice. And those who follow good become
good, and who refuse to know evil
can never know that which is
good."

In *Tasin* 6: 30, Azazil is defined as under:

> "He was named Azazil for he
> chose withdrawal and was
> displaced from his state he had held
> in heaven. His withdrawal is the
> reversion from his essence and is opposed
> to what he really is. And it is made
> bright and aflame for his insistence and
> withdrawal."

In *Tasin* 6:34, Hallaj further says:

> "The Wisemen of the Tribe became
> dumb and mute about him ; and
> those who recognise and had words to
> say become speechless in
> his (Azazil's) plight. . . ."

In these references about Azazil (Iblis), Hallaj is more emphatic on this archetypal character, and only obliquely places the Pharaoh within the ambit of valuation. Azazil supplies a negative form of behaviour, and as such establishes an example of withdrawal. Hallaj is not favourably inclined towards Iblis, and does not have any sympathy for Iblis' withdrawal into his function as Azazil. Still, however, what goes to Azazil's favour is his unflinching identification with the thought-structure which lacks absorption of the attributive totality. In this the Reason becomes self-destroying which indeed is the etymological meaning of the word: *Shaitan* (Satan). Most Hallaj scholars have overlooked the allegorical nature of the characters, and have, therefore, intermixed Hallajian Iblis with its counterpart of the popular tradition.

(19)

In this dramaturgic presentation where Iblis holds the central position, it is in fact Adam who defines Iblis in Hallajian terms. The supremacy of Adam, which is implied in the Divine commandment, suggests subordination of the thought-content which finds expression in Iblis. Iblis, as archetypal character, represents *intellect*, and its conjunction with Adam promises its absorption into the matrix of human feelings. That intellect must germinate in the soil of human feelings in order to know God in His totality. Thus, Adam becomes the real instrument of Divine Knowledge, and Iblis' withdrawal remains onesided and self-consuming. In the dramaturgic presentation it is Adam who shows the possibility of fulfilment of the Divine Will. The central position erstwhile occupied by Iblis is filled by Adam. *Tasin* 6 is in fact the Book of Adam. The Hallajian metaphysics chooses Adam to be the living witness of the Divine Knowledge. With this perspective in view the world of Hallaj emerges in Muslim history, and moves out of the world-picture sketched and pains-takingly elaborated by the Mu'tazilite thinking.

Another important thing which deserves notice is that the main argument of *Tasin* 6, in terms of the Divine Knowledge, is directed towards the Holy Prophet whose blessed presence on the outer limits of the historico-cosmic situation (6 : 1-4) provides content to the Hallajian notion of the Truth. And Adam, while holding the central position in the situation, emerges from his cosmic condition and enters human history precisely on the point where *al-Haqq* (the Truth) is manifest in the revelation of the Holy Prophet. In this wider outline, the archetypal character is negatively projected in the Pharaoh, and by extension rediscovers itself in the personal "I" (6: 23) which is generally ascribed to Hallaj himself. In fact, the personal "I" in 6: 23 is the point which is intersected by Adam and the historical Hallaj in the presence of *al-haqq* which is the Truth of Revelation manifest in the Holy Prophet. Thus, Adam, as Mankind, displaces the particular Hallajian ego, as located in biography, and becomes the Universal Ego to discover *al-Haqq* through the mediation of the Holy Prophet. Otherwise the intra-referential Scheme in *Tasin* 6 would have lost the basis of its argument.

(20)

Set within the background outlined above, the Hallajian expression: *ana al-haqq* occurs in *Tasin* 6:23

in the following context (6: 21-23):

> "And Hallaj said : 'I entered into disputation
> with both Iblis and the Pharaoh
> on unswerving assertion ; on
> Steadfastness ; and Iblis said that
> prostration before Adam was
> disclaiming steadfastness, it would have made
> him alien to himself. And the Pharaoh
> said that the belief in His messenger was
> enough to soil his name
> before his people. And to them I made
> reply that if I too go back upon my own
> faith, I lose my being,
> my station.'
> And then said Iblis . . . 'I am better
> than he [Adam] ; and He had known none
> other than Himself' ; and the Pharaoh said :
> 'I know not—that you have any god but me ;
> and he had no one
> among his people to discriminate ;
> to choose between the truth and the untruth ;
> between the true and
> the false.'
> And I said, 'If you recognise Him not, then
> just see and recognise His
> ever-lasting sign, the ever-enduring sign ;
> and that Sign I am, and I am
> the Truth [*ana al-Haqq*] and within the Reality
> I am for ever
> with the Truth.' "

The dramaturgic presentation with its archetypal characters merges into higher poetry in the situation and experience given above. The archetypal characters draw their intrinsic significance from the personal "I," which in its state of poetic ecstasy enters into high and serious relationship with the Truth. In its context, however, the personal "I" is a symbolisation of the "everlasting sign" and, because of it, the personal "I" defines itself as the Truth—which is an identification, yet it remains as ever in co-extensive state with the Truth. The everlasting sign, in special reference to Iblis and the Pharaoh, is Adam at the moment historically represented by the experiential being externally understandable as Hallaj. This is a vertical station where the personal "I" of the recipient of experience becomes the Universal "I," and as such speaks for Adam who carries the Divine Will in human history.

The ecstasy in its higher poetic state, which forms the essential component of Sufic sensibility, is, in the present instance, the expression of the thought-structure which permeates the earlier books of *Tawasin.* The mind of Hallaj throughout these books is actively involved in questions which are basically meant for a conscious treatment. And in this developing environment the ecstasy, like a spark, emerges from the deeper layers of the conscious mind, and transforms the personal "I," and enters into a renewed relationship with the notion (*al-haqq*) which explains the phenomenon of revelation. The ecstasy confirms the discovery conducted by the thought-structure in *Tawasin.* But even in the state of ecstasy the personal "I" discloses an inner movement which is perhaps overlooked under the charm of the Hallajian expression of *ana al-haqq.* In fact, Hallaj's position within the given experience is centred on the question of Divine Knowledge: the gnosis of God, and it shifts from that reference to the idea of the everlasting sign which is made particular within the personal "I". And the personal "I" is identified with the Truth. This identification is, however, bifurcated, and the personal "I" reappears as an external and objectively related dimension of the truth.

This ecstatic experience, which forms the climax of the *Tawasin* thought-structure, offers a few important observations. Given that Iblis and the Pharaoh, in their cosmic and historical condition, fail to know God in His revelation, Hallaj's assertion and reference towards the "ever-enduring sign" does not equate the Sign with the Divine Notion. Then at this initial stage of Hallajian assertion it is equally important to ask as to what is the exact nature of the "ever-enduring sign" which is capable of authentication of the Divine Notion. In the framework of *Tasin* 6, it is Adam who is the "ever-enduring sign," because he interconnects the eternal scheme of existence with the historical human condition. And, as such, the Divine Will, through Adam, authenticates the Divine Notion. At this moment the entry of the personal "I," in the ecstatic state, imparts a concrete location to the "ever-enduring sign" which has remained latent in the human condition. As an argument the answer supplied by Hallajian ecstatic experience in terms of the "ever-enduring sign" should have stopped at this point. The Sign has in a way authenticated the Notion. But it has not really followed this expectation. On the contrary, the personal "I" had emerged first to activate the Sign and next to orientate the process of authentication towards the Truth. The personal "I" interconnects the Sign with the Truth; it spreads itself across the whole phenomenon of creation (of Man) and Revelation. Textually, the personal "I" appears first as the Sign and next as the Truth, and then disappears into Reality to reappear as an objective condition for authentication of the Truth. Thus, it is the Truth which essentially authenticates the Divine Notion.

(21)

The identification of the personal "I" in serious poetic experience has always remained an important problem of literary thinking. The personal emotion through poetic experience loses its personal reference and is transformed into poetic emotion which loses its identity in biographical terms. The personal "I," likewise, ceases to remain personal and assumes an impersonal character when it passes through poetic experience. Even at the highest level of poetic expression the personal "I" is displaced by an impersonal "I," which, in its turn, echoes the totality of the creative medium and its environment. The impersonal "I," at this level, gives expression to the reactivated environment. Perhaps, such was the phenomenon which impelled the old traditional thinking to ask as to who is the Speaker behind the personal "I" of Hallaj's ecstatic experience. In poetry the personal "I" is frequently changed into the impersonal "I," which, while reacting to various conceptions, gives expression to them through itself. The conceptions speak through the impersonal "I". The phenomenon, however, remains involuntary, and the expression becomes automatic writing.

In its textual context, therefore, the impersonal "I" is the point where the Sign and the Truth meet and impart to it the strength of re-experienced faith. In fact, the Sign itself merges into the Truth, and the impersonal "I" becomes its witness in time. However, the impersonal "I" also shows its textual gradations; the Sign and the Truth are represented by it, and through their mediation the impersonal "I," while moving between Creation and Revelation, lays added emphasis on *al-haqq*. And, while conducting the creative sensibility along these conceptions the impersonal "I" affirms their validity in its immediate and anticipated environment. The ecstatic experience of Hallaj and its emergent impersonal "I" attest the Truth within the framework of Islam. And the Truth, as Revelation, authenticates the Divine Notion.

(22)

In Hallajian world-picture the cry of *ana al-haqq* was raised in an environment which was shattered by the alienation of mind (Intellect/Iblis) and the human condition (the Pharaoh). The way to God was blocked by the dread of His unknowability, and the Truth was equated with logical construction. In this milieu Hallaj was capable of submerging his personal "I," and in extending consciousness to the emerging impersonal

"I". He was, thus, successful in orientating the psycho-physical being towards the Truth revealed in Islam. Hallaj's discovery of the impersonal "I" was in fact the mystery which was not available in explanation to the intellectual climate of the age. He added a new dimension to the idea of the human being, and with this dimension the Muslim history entered a more fruitful and rewarding era of its civilisation. Hallaj saved the Muslim world from collapsing under the threat of a Godless cosmology. He activated the living psychological structure to receive the Revelation in its immediacy and to know God through the mediation of the Truth. For centuries, Hallaj has spoken to Muslims in the idiom of love, and *ana al-haqq* has remained the consoling voice for many generations in the misery of spiritual loneliness. The grandmothers in their folk-tales still talk of Mansur in the far-off homes of the Muslim world. The old men, while looking towards the blue skies, listen to the mystery of *ana al-haqq* and heave sighs of inner distress. And in the silence of the tropical nights the voice of the *Qawwali*-singers fades out into timelessness. *Ana al-haqq; ana al-haqq; ana al-haqq!*

PART II

TAWASIN

HUSAIN BIN MANSUR HALLAJ

Tasin I

BOOK OF LUMINOUS FORM

Thus said Husain b. Mansur Hallaj (may Allah be pleased with him) :

(1) "Tasin . . . ;
it was a shining form of light from the
Unseen, and it appeared and illumined,
and returned to the Unseen, and it
surpassed all lights and became the
light of lights, and its brightness spread
across all the moons. Its
luminous apex has gone up beyond the
skies which are
surrounded by mystery.
Truth named him *Ummi*
to assure him, called him One
of the Sacred House to regard him
in his greatness; and named him
Makki for his fixed and unchanging
station and for the nearness that
he had with
Truth itself.

(2) His breast was undimensioned and his place
was raised
above and his will was made
imperative. He was thus relieved,
relieved of what oppresses. And to all
revealed his moon; and the moon,

his moon came out of the clouds in the land of
Yamamah and became the morning sun in Tahamah, and his lamp
gave light of
Superior Wisdom.

(3) Whatever he said in his wisdom,
in his light, and of the six things he said
he said in the correctness
of his spirit. He first made himself
present, and had insight, and then
himself became the eye that sees; and then
he warned; first
he showed the way, then
put limit on the way.

(4) As Reality none has seen
him, save his friend, Siddiq the True; who
knew him as he knew him; he stood by him;
shared steps with him, and none was there
to separate
them.

(5) And no traveller who seeks
has seen him, nor known him; and none
has recognised him; and his virtue
remained unknown as there was none
to create his
virtue. So, the Truth desired to
unravel the Truth, and those who passed
away had the Book and they
knew him as they knew their sons; and one
among them concedes

the Truth.
(6) From his light appeared
the light of all prophecy, and from
his rays of light
new rays of light appeared. And there is
no other light more bright, and
clearer and
more ancient than his
light.
(7) His meditation surpassed all
meditations and his being transcended
un-being,
and his name excelled
the Pen, for he preceded all people, in
this world or in
some other world or in the world
beyond the world. There is none
so full of charm, and kind and wise
and deep in thought
like him; he is the head of all
created things; he is
Ahmad, and praise belongs to him and
unsurpassed in praise his word
endures as he is generous in his
being and high in his virtue and
unique
in his thought when deep
in thought.
(8) He made him all supreme, above
everything and raised him in his place; and
proclaimed him great and known on

earth and sea; and made him
bright and full of light and
powerful and one
who sees and understands; before the
creation was known he was
already known;
and from first to last his name
remains inscribed on
time. His essence purifies; his word
warns and his knowledge
elevates; his speech is Arab speech, but
his tribe is neither in the east
nor in the west; his race and what
succeeds him
claim esteem; and he has a friend
in the sacred house.

(9) He made a sign and the eyes had
sight and things unknown,
concealed and things mysterious became
known,
familiar things. The Truth made him
speak, the
reason proved him true and then
made him free. He is the manifested
Truth, and the Truth manifests itself in his
Truth manifest. His breast was cleansed of
dark spot. He came, not with a word
invented or constructed or one
that loses form or sense or is the work of
someone here or there—; he came with the
word that changes not, nor follows change;

co-exists in Truth and is outside all
scheme of reason; has told the Cause of
causes and
of End of ends.

(10) And above him flashed the cloud, the
cloud which flashed; and under his feet
the lightning flashed
and darkness ceased; and
the cloud let go its water-drops
as rain; and the earth had
fruit. All knowledge is a tiny drop of water
beside his ocean—;
and all wisdom is a drink
of water from his deep
deep river; and all
that was, and had existence beyond the time
of written time
is just a moment in his
time.

(11) Truth is with him, and what is measured
and what is unmeasured is also with him.
In Presence he is the first and he is
the last in the line of messengers;
he is the hidden meaning of
creation and the
manifest meaning of the knowledge
of the Essence.

(12) But no seeker after knowledge has
reached him, and no giver of
judgment has met his
wisdom.

(13) Truth never took him to things
created for he is he, yet
where is he ? Thus whoever he is,
he is.

(14) And none who knows or who knows
he knows has ever gone beyond the
mim of Muha*m*mad ; there is no way out
for him ; likewise
whoever moves within has never gone beyond
the *hay* of Mu*h*ammad ; the *hay* leads to
the second *mim* ; and the letter
dal brings back to the first *mim*
of Muha*m*mad.

(15) His word revealed ; his warning
came to all and all became dumb
before his word. And the Quran
appeared in revelation, and
spoke in his speech as smooth as ever ; and
illumined his heart and strengthened
its foundation. And those who stood beside
stood thus beside ; and showed
his word as true and
proclaimed his greatness
as greatness.

(16) If you leave and escape to land away
from him you will find no way, and none
to own you.
O sick in soul, you will see no one to
save you. The wise talk of the Wisest of
the world is like sand-hills before him.

Tasin II

BOOK OF THE WAY

(1) The created being
can hardly know the Real; and the Real
has no contact with the
thought and thinking of the things
created. What enters the heart is the fleeting
wave of thought, and this and that and
so many waves of thought
can never reach the
Real. So far it is, its knowledge. So, how to
know the Real?
Truth is beyond Reality—as something
unidentified and Reality is apart from
Truth.

(2) The candlemoth hangs around the light
of the candle, all night and
in different forms returns with the
morning sun,
in the morning; and then relates
what happened, how it happened; and in what
happened lies joy, his only
happiness; for his breast contains the hope
to meet
perfection.

(3) The light shed by Flame is the
knowledge of Reality and its warmth
suggests the Real that lies within that

knowledge; but to enter its warmth and to
know its light thereby is
Truth.

(4) The candlemoth is not pleased with
the light of the candle, with the
warmth of the candle; so he throws itself
in the flame of the candle; and different
Forms
await the candle-moth's return; thus, he
gives news, informs of
what he saw or how he lived
through it. The candle-moth just prefers
his seeing to
what is heard; and thus becomes
non-being, a thing of worthless stuff,
fragmented. Then, in the present form
he ever lives, without name,
without form or body, without sign
or symbol.
You ask me why?
for what he had such different forms? And
how he reached the state? for what?
for what?
Who reached the state of seeing, became
indifferent to the state of hearing, of news, of
love transmitted; who finds access to him,
who is being observed goes far beyond
the state of sight, of
observation.

(5) But he who is given to instincts
and their desires, and who is

weak in thought and who wears sin as
dress for mortal life, will never meet
success, like me.

(6) O, if you think that I am
one who has reached that state or
who will ever reach that state,
or had reached that state sometime
in the past, O, never, never, never!
I am on my way to His discovery, on my
way that leads to Him. O, I belong to
Him and He does not own me yet.

(7) O!
If you want to know then know that
what is Real is known to none
save Ahmad; and Muhammad is not the
father of any of your men but
the Apostle of God and the Last of the
Apostles of God. And when he
went beyond this world and that,
the world beyond and passed beyond the
place of
Men and Jinn, and unknown to
Men and Jinn, there lurked no more, any sign
or speck of error; and then he
approached and came closer, and was
at a distance of but two bowlengths or
nearer.
And when he reached the Real
its knowledge, the state of knowledge where
what is
Real is known he made his own

heart its news, and left aspiring.
When reached the Truth, far off the Real,
and placed himself before Him Who is
Merciful, and when the Truth was made his
own he turned back and said: My mind
has none but you, prostrates for you;
my heart belongs to you.
And as he reached the End of
ends he said: No words there are to
circumscribe, no language to define
you; and when he reached the Real of
the real,
he said: You are indeed as you have said; he
let go all that lives in mortal world, and
reached the Throne, and his heart
in no way falsified that which he saw; and
near the Tree that marked the bounds of
knowledge, and beyond which no one passes,
his sight never swerved nor did it
go wrong!

Tasin III

BOOK OF INFORMATION

(1) Reality is sharp and edged; the way to it
is narrow with flames of burning fire, high and
low, of all description; and far beyond
there lies a field of
wilderness, dark and unfrequented; the
stranger walks through it and covers a
chain of forty states and
tells what happens
there.

(2) For each state there are
modes of thought, their sciences, some easy
to learn, far easy to understand; and
some beyond and far beyond
understanding.

(3) And, then, he—
the stranger enters the field of wilderness and
settles there and moves beyond; he owns
no one and loves
no one; the way is covered in
moment's time; the hills, the rocks, the
perilous
crests of hills, nor land, how rough,
how smooth,
can stay him on his way.

(4) And when Moses had fulfilled the
term he left his family and Reality was

his family; he was content with what he
knew, had heard; preferred transmission
to that observed; for this made him and
the Best of Men two different men; and
distinguished the high and low. He, thus
addressed:
Perhaps I came to you with news from
there.

(5) And when the man who
leads agrees to bare report, to heard,
transmitted
news, then those
who follow steps betake themselves to
seek relief in sign
and symbol.

(6) On Mount Sinai, the Tree! And
what was heard was heard from there;
or someone else, manifested
there.

(7) And thus I stand as Tree; and what
I say is not my word, his
word.

(8) Thus, what is Real is
real and that belongs to things
created is thing created; so give up things
created to
be as he and you as he, and this is
what is Real.

(9) And I see the attribute, and the
attributed himself relates the
attribute; and, thus, contains the Real within

himself; so who he is?
(10) And Truth replied: When you thus
move in thought and prove; the Proved One
never proved. As I stand
open proof.
(11) Truth let me see the Real by
affirmation, by covenant,
by word of mouth; and what I knew
spoke out in spite of what I had in
my heart—, the secret that I have
transcends
Reality.
(12) Truth told me about my heart, and gave
me knowledge in my own
tongue, and held me close; my otherness
ceased,
and I became its
own.

Tasin IV

BOOK OF THE CIRCLE

(1) First circle in the world of appearances is that which leads toward him, and the second circle is that which reached him and cracked; and the third circle is that which entered Reality and lost its way in the wilderness. And by the first circle it is possible to reach him; but through the second circle all lose their way; and in the third circle are woods and deserts and extended wilderness.

(2) Alas! for him who entered the first circle and found it blocked, and was asked to retrace his steps. In this state there co-exist one's essence, thought and wonderment.

(3) No opening is there in the first circle; but see the point in the heart of the circle—; Reality is that point of the circle.

(4) And what is Reality? It does not

annihilate things, either apparent or
abstract; whether
seen by eyes or recognised by the
soul; and then,
these never change; and have new forms.

(5) If you want to know and
understand what I have said, then
take four birds, and tame them to turn
to you; for
Truth never flies.

(6) His otherness makes
him present in his absence, but his
power obstructs and
wonderment
deprives.

(7) These are the meanings of
Reality; yet finer and sharper are the
meanings when you suspend
your judgment and bitterly
long for
meaning.

(8) He looks on all sides of
the circle but never sees beyond
it.

(9) And the knowledge of
Reality is also pure and sacrosanct and the
circle
is the circle of
sanctity.

(10) For this, he was named
pure and sacrosanct, and has never

come out of the circle
of sanctity.
(11) And He is still
beyond, across whatever is; so, he
heaved the sigh of
inaccessibility.

Tasin V

BOOK OF THE POINT

(1) And far more perilous and deep
is the discourse about the
Point; it is the essence which neither
grows nor
fades, nor
ceases to exist.
(2) Whoever disbelieves, says no, negates
the Point, belongs
to the first circle, of appearances; so—
when he saw me not,
he disbelieved in my state and said I am
one of those who worship
Fire, and have faith in duality, and, thus,
made me
hateful.
(3) But—that of the second circle saw
me in the state where
the Sustainer
sustains.
(4) And who reached the third circle said:
I am in the grip
of aspirations.
(5) And he, who reached the circle of
Reality, knew nothing of me, and vanished
before me, in the
Unseen.

(6) There is no place to
take refuge; by no means! no place of safety; before
thy Lord that day will be the place of
rest; that day will man be told that he put forward, and all
that he put back.

(7) And he goes for report transmitted, and
for heard news, for things that are heard, conveyed
from one to other, and seeks refuge and
fears the spark . . ., deceived, has
plunged in fire, in grave
danger.

(8) And I was one of the two birds kept
by the Sufis; and it had
two wings; and when it could fly
no more, it denied my state.

(9) And then it questioned me: What
is Purity? And I replied: Cut off your
wings with the sharp edge of
non-being; without this you cannot follow
me, know me.

(10) And he said: I fly with my wings,
and I replied: Alas! alas!
how poor you are! for none
resembles him, no similitude there is, of
him, and still he hears and
sees. On that day he
fell in the ocean of meaning, into the
sea of understanding and

sank.

(11) And what is the visible form of meaning;
of understanding; it is the
circle.
I saw my Lord with the eye, my
inner eye, and asked: Who art Thou ? and
he replied: You! So, nay is for the where?
and where has no whereness
without you and there is no
where either; and thou art as thou art! And
there is no ultimate judgment in the
world about you; and no judgment has thus
far discovered:
Where art thou? And you have spread
yourself
upon everywhere, and where has
lost its whereness. So, where art thou ?
Thou? where thou art?

(12) The first point is
in the circle drawn by the power of
judgment; one of them is true,
the other false.

(13) And he passed the night spread
over his heart; and he came nearer and
nearer to his Lord; and
disappeared. And when he saw me,
he disappeared not; and
how he appeared? he appeared not; and
how seen? never seen!

(14) He entered the plane of wonder, and
contemplated; and as he contemplated his

wonder
increased; and he was himself
observed; and afterwards
he deserved himself; he, first, had reunion
but separation a moment
later; his aspiration fell within access, but
was separated from his own
heart. And whatever he saw his heart
denied it
not.

(15) First he concealed and then took him
nearer; gratification first and then
purified; cured him first and then raised
him with care, and purified him; and
gave him the state of glory. And then
made him
suffer and cured him, and
then became his protector and preserved
him, and made him
ride the spheres as heavenly rider.

(16) And he first became the closest, closer
than two bowlengths, and then
observed; and was consistent in act and
in his form. And when he was called he
responded; and when he
meditated, disappeared.
He had his drink of water, and was
contented. And, closer he drew himself, was
overawed, and he left his land,
his friends, companions, helpers—all; and
transcended

all secrets, all mysteries and
all symbols.

(17) Your companion is neither astray, nor being misled. Neither has he fallen ill nor suffered loss of hope; his eye had no temptation for where? And his duration, while in but two bowlengths of distance, knew no sorrow.

(18) Your companion is neither astray nor being misled; and has never gone astray in the garden of recollection, while observing Us; and has never lost his way in the swiftness of thoughtful meditation.

(19) Had every moment in Truth and for Truth; in recollection; and was ever grateful for sorrows and blessings.

(20) It is no less than inspiration sent down to him; and it is light, a sequence of light from end to end.

(21) Gave meaning to the word, beyond judgment, and
it vanished; and detached
himself from whatever
created, from things and men; and became love
of love and said: You be the Bird of the
highest mountains and of the
deepest caverns in the highest mountains;

and the highest
mountains are the heights of meaning;
and the deepest caverns are the
depths of peace and consolation, so that
you may
see what you are destined to see, and
then be
the sharpest sword of affirmation drawn
from the
sacred house.

(22) And then he came nearer to the essence, to
the Meaning; and then he was a
limit to the distance; and then through
states and stages he moved and
approached in persistent quest; came swiftly
down, and went closer as one who is
called; and
came down; and came closer as one
responding; and
came down as one who is closer; and came
nearer as one who witnesses, and as
one who sees,
and came down as one who saw and as one
who witnessed; he came back
to all.

(23) Thus, he became the idea of
the distance of but two bowlengths;
the question
where? was thereby shattered with the
arrow of separation; and the distance of
aloofness was resolved for ever. All this,

to correct
the question where? and to demonstrate
Reality's dissolution in
overpowering Essence.

(24) And this I apprehend. Only he would
understand this,
and all this, who has
drawn the Second Bow; he would only
understand.
And the Second Bow is other than
the Tablet.

(25) And it has other words, beside the
Arabic tongue.

(26) Yet there is one single letter, common to
all; and it is "m".

(27) And "m" is the name of the Last of
all.

(28) And he is the chord of the First Bow.

(29) And he said (may Allah be pleased with him):
The art of the word lies in its nearness, in the
nearness of its meaning; so, the meaning is the
better way for Reality to
approach Truth; it is not safe for all and
sundry; nearness begets the circle of
restraint.

(30) Then, what is Reality? A point where the
links with world contingent exist no
more, its pains, and pangs and
sorrow come back
no more.
It guides and explains; is a word for

salvation;
it leads by a particular way, and
is agreeable to all; and nearness keeps
the meaning
known only to him who
knows; and he is one who is loyal and tried
wayfarer on the Path to
the Apostle; to the Messenger of
Allah.

(31) The Ruler of the city of Yathrib has
said of him, who is safe within the
Book Preserved; and the same is said
in the Books written, and
in the Books seen, and in the
Books that interpret the speech of Birds; and
We have got him there at a distance
of but two bowlengths or nearer, so that he
makes the Essence
the object of his sight.

(32) O Seeker! if you wish to know, then
know full well that no Master condescends
to speak to him who does not deserve
his speech; all dialogue is between the
deserved and
the deserving or with him who
talks and speaks of them.

(33) He does not have a teacher; he neither has
a pupil or disciple, nor has he any
authority nor
discrimination. He betrays none, nor he
warns anyone;

he is not accompanied, either with
thing or person, and neither thing nor person
accompanies
him. And true it is that what he
possesses he only possesses; he may have
it, or
he may have it not; it is always there. He is
a wilderness within the wilderness; he is a
Sign within the sign.

(34) Only he can claim the Meaning, for the
meaning
draws hope only from him. But the hope is
distant and far off, and way to it is rough and
full of dangers; his name is written in
glory, his impression unique in all
respects, and
his recognition is in his
common recognition, and his commonness is
the Reality,
by which he is recognised; his value, his
strength, his
promise, our covenant; his name, his way,
his sign, his fire and the desire for
him, is the only
virtue, the only sign to know him, to
recognise him.

(35) His Name is the name of all praise, and all
the Suns of the Universe are the
light of his Universe, his very field; and all
the men and all the towns and
cities, and the

places where men and women live are
like one House, one Family; his life and being
are not unknown, his state is self-absorbed;
and
when he manifests he turns non-being. Oh,
joy is
the field of roses, his garden; and the
ways made to walk upon, are his
foundations.

(36) Those who help him, and go with
him belong to the tribe of love and are known
by the sign of love; his act is kindness
and his
will is all well known; those who follow him
meet
destination. Yet, his sorrow is great; things
about him slow-paced, and silent and
quiet pain,
unceasing.

(37) Whatever he said is said forever; it is
always so, always there. And this the
glory, and
this is what assures; all else is
going astray into
ignorance, into
wilderness, without way, without end,
without
destination.

Tasin VI

BOOK OF ADAM

On the Interpretation of Meaning and Whatever Has Been Said Its Affirmation in that Light

Thus said the greatest Teacher and Master (may Allah in His Mercy purify his spirit) :

(1) And there is none to have
said He is: The One,
except Ahmad, and peace be upon
him, and to him alone has He
appeared in vision within
vision.
Iblis stood blocked in his own being.

(2) Iblis was commanded to prostrate; and
Ahmad (peace be upon him) was asked to
see; and Ahmad (peace be upon him) neither
looked to the right, nor
towards the north; his sight never swerved,
nor did it go
wrong.

(3) Iblis claimed but could not free
himself of whatever he was made, and of
himself.

(4) And Ahmad (peace be upon him)
claimed, and stepped beyond the finite and
the self, and made no
compromise.

(5) And showed thereby, and kept the word;
I move through you, and through you
cover, whatever is. And thus:
O mover of all hearts! who can
tell Your glory and praise
You?

(6) And there was none in the skies, superior to
Iblis, who knew the One as ONE....

(7) And Iblis deflected in the Being, he
gave up sight and observation, and
abandoned
the journey through being; abandoned
to observe. He worshipped God as
Divine Abstract,
Abstraction.

(8) And when he reached the stage of
individuation, he stood
condemned; and when he passed beyond
the stage
and begged for it, he was brought
into Presence.

(9) He was commanded to prostrate; and he
said: "There is none other than You.
Said: "You
are condemned." He said:
"There is none other than You."

(10) My deflection is the outcome of Your
transcendence, of Your Purity; and
my reason is my madness for You. I
know none but You, and Adam is none but
other than You. In between You and I, there

none exists; if aught exists, it is
I.

(11) "For me there is no way to what is
other than You; and I am of their side
who side with reason, and who go for
reason." Said: "You raised yourself
too high."
Replied: "Then, only then; had I compared
myself with
You—, then pride it was, my raising of
myself
within myself . . .; and it was none else
but I who knew You in pre-existence,
in time before time. In preference
I come before anyone else as I stayed
perpetually
in obedience before any of Your creation
did ever knew obedience. Thus, Your
knowing is
mine, and in inclination, You lean
towards me and I do lean towards You.
And this
our leaning between us is far far ancient
than ancient time itself. So, why should I
prostrate before one who is not You but
other than You. And so—deflection;
there was
no choice, no way, no other
act left but what I did. The fire which gave
me form attracts me back to
fire. And fire begets fire. The will is

Yours; and whatever You now
determine is, as ever,
Yours.

(12) "In separation from You there is no other
aloofness
left for me; and I realise that far and near
are simple words—
without content; for I have gone so far and
away from You. And I have made
separation from You
my friend—, companion in my plight.
And who could name it such,
though it be love, and just appear
estrangement from You."

(13) And Moses met Iblis in the
wilderness of Sinai—and asked: "What
kept you
back from prostration?" Replied: "This
firm conviction
that He is One and the only One; had I
prostrated before Adam, I would have
changed
with you; that you were called to look
toward the hill, and you
obeyed. And I was called a thousand times to
prostrate before Adam but my
firm conviction
came in my way."

(14) Said: "You disobeyed command";
replied: "A
trial it was, no command." Said:

"It changed your Form." Replied:
"O Moses! all this
is meant to hide, to cover and keep
under cover whatever there is
to cover; and now what use? for what is
"is" and
that what is
changes. And that which does not change is
the true knowledge; the same it was on
that
day, and the same it is now
today. The real being has not undergone
the change."

(15) And Moses said: "Still remember Him?"
Replied:
"Why? all remembrance and contemplation
is one and the same. I am still the
same who is being remembered; and even
He is
being remembered. Thus His remembrance is
mine and mine His; and do the two be
One? United in the
moment? I am clean now in my
serving days, and my days are my own
days, and
His thought within my thought is
brighter than before. And then I served
Him to my
joy and now I serve Him to
His joy.

(16) "And there is no more thought of

recompense;
of loss or gain; has made me
unreplaceable, and in this state I stay
as ever;
and made me see and wonder; and then,
and then,
renounced that I may not be found
with those who are free, released and without
bondage. And for my transgression
kept me back from others, and gave me
different shape
to confuse me in my
confusion. All this to prolong my way and
to deepen my
confusion. He held me in confinement as His
own, and for the praise I had, He
let me fall. Has held me far from Himself
for the
act which was my
act, and deprived me of the
power of sight, of
observation. As I was nearer Him, He gave
me freedom;
and as I moved apart,
He held me in His view, and took back
hope, and made me
thus forsaken; far and away from
all.

(17) "And I did not err
in acts determined or in non-determined
acts; or in going against

the will; nor have I felt some pride in
the change of my Form. If He kept me in
fire, from end to end, I will not
bow; will never, never prostrate before
man, for I only bow
to Him; for no one, nor for any form or
shape or person; I know
only Him. I stand with the true, and by
my love,
I am one of them."

Thus said Husain b. Mansur Hallaj (may Allah be pleased with him):

(18) Many are the views about Azazil;
he is the one who warns in the heaven
and on the earth; on the sky
he bade the angels see whatever be
good, and on the earth he bade
man see the evil; and good is
known by its opposite and evil is
known by what contradicts it.

(19) The fine silken cloth is made by the
coarse thread taken from rude and
coarse cloth. In the same manner
the King brings forth the things good
and the things evil, and suggests
choice. And those who follow good become
good, and who refuse to know evil
can never know that which is
good.

Thus said Husain b. Mansur Hallaj (may Allah be

pleased with him), the greatest Teacher of all times:

(20) And Hallaj said: "I entered into disputation
with both Iblis and Pharaoh
on unswerving assertion; on
steadfastness; and Iblis said that
prostration before Adam was
disclaiming steadfastness, it would have made
him alien to himself. And Pharaoh
said that belief in His messenger was
enough to soil his name
before his people. And to them I made
reply.

(21) If I too go back upon my own
faith, I lose my being,
my station.

(22) And then said Iblis . . . "I am better
than Adam; and He had known none
other than Himself"; and Pharaoh said:
"I know not—that you have any god but me;
and he had no one
among his people to discriminate;
to choose between the truth and the untruth;
between the true and
the false."

(23) And I said: "If you recognise Him not, then
just see and recognise His
everlasting sign, the ever-enduring sign;
and that Sign I am, and I am
*the Truth**, and within Reality

---

* *Ana al-Haqq.*

I am for ever
with the Truth."

(24) So, Iblis and Pharaoh are my
friends and by them I find my way; fire
met Iblis, yet he never diverged from
what he held; and Pharaoh went under
water, and
drowned, yet never had his thought
dismantled.
But Pharaoh said: "I believe there is no god
except
Him Whom the children of Israel
believe in; I am of those who
submit." And have you not seen the sign of
God, when Gabriel
made Pharaoh touch the sand in the
depth of water?

(25) If I be killed or put alive on gibbet
or my hands and feet cut off,
even then I will never go back
on my word.

(26) Iblis is the name of his state; it changed
into Azazil.

(27) And it was said to
him: "O, who has fallen! would you never
prostrate?" Replied: "I am one of those who
love, and those who love are cursed. And you
say I have gone down; have fallen; ah, I
who has drawn knowledge
from the book of light—O all-powerful!
how it befell? why it befell—? O, how to

face what I have to face?
You made me of fire, and him of clay; and
we two are mutually opposite; can the
opposites be reconciled?
In obedience and in serving you I am the
most ancient, in partaking of your
love I am the most acknowledged; in
knowing I am the wisest; and in time
I am the most
enduring."

(28) And to him the most High replied:
"All freedoms are Mine, not yours." He said,
and the same is my position; my everything is
Yours; freedom, liberty—all. O my Creator!
so this is
ordained for me? You made me not to
prostrate by Your
will, and You are all-powerful, most high.
If I have erred in my words, then
leave me not; for You are all-knowing,
all-hearing. And had You willed prostration,
I would have prostrated. And none else is
among the travellers on the Path who
knows better than I; I know and
understand.

(29) And, denounce me not, for denunciation
is not the proper recompense. O Lord, my
God! compensate
me for I am unreplaceable in my
faith. In all promises Your word is the most
true, and my act is the most grievous, yet

who wants to know may know that I
am the best of
the witnesses.

(30) O my brother! so this was how he had
his name: Azazil; he detached himself; and
lost his place; and has not reached the end
as there was no beginning; in fact, without
beginning he is still
in the end.

(31) His coming out is an inversion; inversion
of his essence, which is burnt by the
fire of his unbending
zeal; and is brightened by the light of his
detachment.

(32) O my brother! by understanding this
you saved
yourself, or you had met
detachment, separation, sorrow; and
bitterness, and death in
sharp regrets.

(33) The Wisemen of the Tribe became
dumb and mute about him; and
those who recognised, and had words to
say became speechless in
his plight. He knew the meaning of
prostration; and he was the most near to
Him; and
he was the most loyal in his
faith, before his
Creator.

(34) And they prostrated before Adam; they

obeyed. Iblis refused, for he was blinded by
his observation.

(35) And, at last, when he had
come to nought; his expectations ended; he
said: "I am better than he," and for ever
remained in
state of detachment, unreconciled; was lost in
the dust, and faced
suffering from end to
end.

Tasin VII

BOOK OF DIVINE WILL

(1) The first circle is the circle of His
Will; the second circle is the circle of His
Wisdom; the third circle is the circle of His
Power; the fourth circle is the circle of His
Knowledge and of ever-livingness.

(2) Iblis said: "If I entered the first circle, there
was death in the second; and if in the
second, there was death in the third; if I
stopped in the third, there was
still death
there. So . . .

(3) "No, no, no, no, no . . . , I stopped
at the first circle, and was cursed from the
second; and I was thrown into the third; and
lost the fourth. Where is the fourth circle? the
fourth circle!

(4) "Had I known prostration will
release me, set me free, I would have
prostrated before Adam. But I knew of circles
within circles . . . without end. So,
I said in my heart—forgive me! forgive me!
If I could only come out of it, of this
first circle. Even this, yet what about circles,
other circles?

(5) "Ah! the One, the only One, who ever
is. How? how? how?"

Tasin VIII

BOOK OF DIVINE UNITY

(1) Truth is one, unique, single; it is indivisibly One.

(2) And its Oneness, and the knowledge of that oneness belongs to him; is placed in him.

(3) Impossible, impossible; it is aloofness, estrangement, separation; he is known only by them.

(4) Knowledge of One is abstract; single, indivisible.

(5) To say one, and to say single is to reach the attribute; but he, who is one, is beyond attribute.

(6) If I say "I," he sends back "I," in answer to my "I". So, "he" is for you and not for me.

(7) And if I say Unity is Oneness for his loneliness, for his being alone, then I placed him in creation; among things created.

(8) And if I say single One, as number one; how can he come within number?

(9) And if I say, he is One for as the result of being considered one, being proved

One—then I
placed limit on him; delimited
him.

Tasin IX

BOOK OF MYSTERY

(1) All mystery begets awe; it leads
to him, for he has made it move, step by step,
and phase by phase.

(2) The secret of His oneness lies in the
reference by pronouns; He is all concealed,
hidden;
even hidden within the
hidden. He is the personal I; he is also the
absent he; the pronoun of
non-presence.

(3) If you say: Ha, all men say ah!
ah! ah!

(4) How many ways, how many forms, and
how many are the
hints
indicating him; still he is all
unknown.

(5) Like a strong rock.
And this is the limit, and still the limit
does not make him one, as what is limited
is ever limited; and his attributes lead to
limitation; while who is One is ever
beyond
limitation.

(6) *Al-Haqq* is the place of return for
Haqq; in no way

Haqq
itself.
(7) And has he ever said: I am One; and is not
what is said, and
what becomes
a phenomenon, a matter of creation? So, how
do these define
the Truth?
(8) And, if this is said that he himself
said he is one, then
the being depends on act; and what is
created is being. But Being is not the being
though it
has being; still it is
no-being.
(9) He hides himself when most apparent. But
where? And where is the spot
where he
never is?
(10) What? and this. Can never have
him.
(11) As this and where? are his creations.
(12) What is contingent presupposes the
essence; and
what is not without form
or body has
form or body; and what is not without the
spirit
is never
without the spirit.
(13) We back return to that which gathers all,

things added, numbered;
things known and recognised,
things shattered, broken, shaken, and
fragmented;
all.

(14) The first things are things of the act; the
others exist as points on the
circles which mark
the world and its
universe.

(15) When we talk of Divine Unity we talk
of the way toward it; of its directions,
dimensions;
and it is different,
independent, and
a circle by itself.

Tasin X

BOOK OF TRANSCENDENCE

(1) And it is the circle; that is the
form, its form.
(2) And it is a thing of numbers, followed
by men in all ages, in all lands; followed by
men of different ways, and of different
habits of mind, and of
heart.
(3) The first circle gives the things of
appearances; the second gives those that
touch
the non-apparent, the inner and the
innermost.
(4) And all these are
creations: moving, revolving, excited, and
impulsive; interlinked, inverted,
confused, broken, and
fragmented.
(5) And move in the orbit, in the
twilight of human conscience; with anxiety,
bewildered, struck with wonder, and
ever-changing;
and unhappy, and for ever
wandering in valleys; from valley to valley.
(6) These, and these are things
created, things that vary from moment to
moment; the

Truth transcends them all; is free of these
things,
is pure; beyond the
reach of human fantasy.

(7) And if I say He is, they will not enter
argument about His unity or about His
Oneness,

(8) And if I say that it is manifest; is
known, is obvious; they just respond and say:
"It is true."

(9) And if I say it is beyond Time, they make
retort by saying: "It is immanent"; and
what is
immanent can never hold the attributes of the
Truth. They never contemplate on Truth, nor
on that
which is contingent and falls under
things created; for numbers bring limitation.
And if what is One, and what is Oneness
is added
or increased by number, then One
becomes a thing emerging from non-being;
and
Truth is far beyond it. The Being, the Truth
is One
and only One, and what is true
and what is untrue have no relation
with Essence, Being Supreme, or
Truth.

(10) And if I say the One, its Unity . . . is the
word revealed; the word revealed is none

but the
attribute of Being.

(11) And if I say: "He wished it to be One"; the will, the act become just attributes; and whatever is desired or whatever is willed belongs to things created; becomes contingent, a form of willed creation.

(12) And if I say: Allah is the Being, the Essence; the Being transcends, becomes the higher One, the only One.

(13) And if I say: He is no Being; I then count him as creation.

(14) And if I say: The Name and the Named are One, then the oneness comes to nought.

(15) And if I say: He is Allah, and Allah He, then Allah ideates Allah; and He remains as He.

(16) And this is the state where causation is negated; and it is the state that manifests; and circles form new circles with the known towards unknown.

(17) The first circle gives beginning, of things; the second of things of thought, of understanding; the

third begets dimensions; and the fourth
sums up
the known.

(18) Without attributes the Essence, the Supreme
Being remains unknown;
incomprehensible.

(19) He first comes through the door, the door of
knowledge, and does not see; and then
from that which
purifies; and does not see; and then
from understanding, and does not see. And
then he
enters by the door, the door of
pure concepts; but
does not see. So, neither being,
nor act, nor word, nor
what is it?
accompany on the way.

(20) All praise to Him Who far transcends the
men of knowledge, and
the men of sight, their thought and their
grasp by His
glory.

(21) And this is the state of negation and also of
affirmation; and it is the state that manifests;
its form is one of
image.

(22) The first image is simple thought; shared
by all; the second is thought by few and
it begets
the circle which gives the

Truth.

(23) All men who come and go have
waters of opinion for their thought; their
thinking sinks in them, in these waters; the
thought
of the few, selected ones, swims over
the waters, on the waters of reason and
understanding.
But these waters dry up, the way becomes a
beaten way, and they are heard no more; their
worlds perish; their arguments lose
prestige, and their knowledge
comes to nothing.

(24) And in the domain of true knowledge,
only
the Merciful subsists; *al-Rahman* subsists;
and all other things become
non-things; it is most pure; and needs no
being and no becoming; and it
transcends; its presence true and deep;
and its
power all-embracing. All glory
rests with Him.
How do we know Him? No beginning and
no end, no limit, neither numbers
have access to His
glory; Creator of all creation, He is known
only
by Himself; He raises and forgives;
and brings forms and souls together
from non-being.

Tasin XI

BOOK OF DISCOVERY*

Thus said Husain b. Mansur Hallaj (may Allah in His Mercy purify his spirit):

(1) The Unknown lies in the quality, the
quality of the seeker; and what is not
known is
the form of the state of the seeker. Thus His
knowledge lies beyond the limits of reason, of
the range of the intellect; therefore
unknown, and
not known. How? never helps; and in the
valleys of Reality
where? has no place. To comprehend the
unlimited
is not the range or quality of that,
which is limited.

(2) It is beyond thought, beyond
contemplation, beyond the world of senses,
beyond
reason and its arguments.

(3) It is beyond annihilation, annihilation of
self.

(4) It is beyond the finite being, beyond the
self contained in the being.

(5) And he who says he has known Him by not

* *Bustan al-Ma'rifah.*

knowing Him is ignorant; and ignorance is a veil of unknowing.

(6) And he who says he has known Him by His Name has known Him not, for how can you discriminate the Name and
the Named?

(7) And he who says he has known Him by
Him, he has
known Him not; for how can the known become unknown? And the two can
ever
co-exist?

(8) And he who says he has known Him by His
Works,
he has known Him not, for he has placed His works in place of
Him.

(9) And then, who says he has known Him in his human helplessness, he is helpless in
himself,
and can never claim
access.

(10) By awareness, and by knowledge you reach nowhere; whatever you get is just the outcomc of
your thought.

(11) By attributes? No, never; for attributes are mere signs, and symbols; they just suggest.

(12) By birth and death, two points on graph of life; how can He thus appear in

graph of life, in two extremes?

(13) Who seldom knows the why and how of things; and
who never knows why mortal frame
is once in youth and then in eld; the black hair on it
is soon replaced by grey; how can he know the
Maker, the Lord Creator of things, of everything?
From this to that,
how possible?

(14) The heart of man is a piece of flesh; it
throbs in the hollow of the
human breast, a point in space. How can He
come within that space?

(15) For the galloping steed, called Reason, there are lengths and
breadths; and for the scheme of life,
the limits of sacred law; and the
whole creation, in the sky and
on the earth, is in state of
His encirclement.

(16) The lengths and breadths can never
reach Him; and His Recognition can hardly
stay within encirclement of
earth and sky; and the things of outer
life and of inner life, of the sacred Law
can scarcely know Him.

(17) If you claim to have known Him by study,
by studying the physical world, through laws, and

signs, you raised yourself much higher;
much higher than the thing
discovered.

(18) Beware, beware! O man in quest of
Truth!
your state decides your state; your
knowing is
half-knowing; your understanding
deserves no praise; so, the true seeker is he
who sees, and true knowledge is that
which stays.

(19) The knowledge based on limits,
on restricted and finite beings extends, but
hides
itself in the state where the Being Supreme
appears in the letter *m*; and
He remains concealed, apparent, and
concealed;
draws near, and back returns. But he, who
moves
within and fears, and
lives in great desire, in love for Him, in
state of separation, remains
in front of Him.

(20) True man of knowledge, the man of
true knowledge is all alone, and he who
loves Him
lives in sorrow; and he who lives for Him
loses all; and
he who has his eyes closed sees Him
in his eyes; His hands

give him support and
sustenance.

(21) Then, what is the true knowledge? It is as
it is. And what is He? He is as He is;
thus, true
knowledge is as He is; and He is as the
true knowledge is. He is He; and
He is, as ever, He.

(22) Whatever is, besides this, is the work of raw
men; the stories told by men in their urge for
stories. True knowledge is the quest of the
few; all other
men live a life of
care. They pick up views and enter confusion;
they
live in self-absorption and give up hope. Their
acts become indifferent, and they
pass their days
in aimlessness, in the dark world of
confusion.

(23) The True remains the True, the Creator
as Creator, and what belongs to things
created,
remains as things created. This
always is; it brings no harm.

PART III

SELECTED BIBLIOGRAPHY

BY

MUHAMMAD IKRAM CHAGHATAI

SELECTED BIBLIOGRAPHY*

European:

(1) 'Abd al-Sabūr, Salāh: Murder in Baghdad (Mas'at al-Ḥallāj). Prize-winning verse play in two acts. Translated with an introduction by I.H. Khalil Semaan. Leiden: Brill, 1972.

(2) Anawati, G. C. et L. Gardet : Mystique musulmane; aspects et tendances; expériences et techniques. Paris: Vrin, 1961.

(3) Arnaldez, R. : Ḥallāj ou la religion de la Croix. Paris: Plon, 1964.

(4) Corbin, H. : Histoire de la philosophie islamique. Paris: Gallimard, 1964.

(5) Gardet, L. : Expériences mystiques en terres non-chrétiennes. Paris: Alsaita, 1954.

(6) ——— : Thèmes et textes mystiques. Paris : Alsaita, 1958.

(7) ——— : La mystique. Paris: P.U.F., 1970.

(8) ——— : Etudes de philosophie et de mystique comparées. Paris: Vrin, 1972.

(9) Gauthier, L. : "El-Hallādj et le Panthéisme" in: Revue de l'histoire des religions, (Paris) 91 (1925), 77—96.

---

* Specially prepared for this Edition by Muhammad Ikram Chaghatai. For a complete bibliography on Husain b. Mansur Hallaj, and a comprehensive study of his life and works, see Chaghatai's article in Urdu Literary Magazine "Sawera", vol. 50—2, May 1976, pp. 89—154.

(10) Goldziher, I.: "Al-Ḥallāj", in: Der Islam, 4 (1913), 165–9.

(11) Horten, M.: "Grundlinien von Lebenssystem und mystischer Weltanschauung des Ḥallāj," in: Archiv fuer Geschichte der Philosophie, 8 (1926), 161—80.

(12) ———— : "Philologische Nachpruefung von Uebersetzungsversuchen mystischer Texte des Ḥallaj," in: Zeitschrift der Deutschen Morgenlaendischen Gesellschaft (Leipzig) N.S. 7 (82, 1928), 23—41.

(13) Lammens, H.: "Al-Hallag, une mystique musulman au IIIe siècle de l'Hégire," in: Recherches de science religieuse (Paris), 5 (1914), 123—35.

(14) Massignon, Louis: La Passion de Husayn Ibn Mansūr Ḥallāj; martyr mystique de l'Islam exécute à Bagdad le 26 mars 922. Etude d'histoire religieuse (Nouvelle édition). Paris: Gallimard, 1975.
Vol. I : "La vie de Ḥallāj," 708 p.
Vol. II : "La survie de Ḥallāj," 519 p.
Vol. III : "La doctrine de Ḥallāj," 386 p.
Vol. IV : "Bibliographie; Index," 331 p.
With maps and illustrations.

(15) ———— : Essai sur les origines du lexique technique de la mystique musulmane. Paris: Geuthner, 1922. Nouvelle édition revue et considérablement augmentée, Paris: Vrin, 1954 (Réimpression, 1968).

(16) Massignon, Louis : Opera Minora (=OM). Textes recueilles classes et presentes avec une bibliographie par Y. Moubarac. 3 vols., Liban : Dar al-Maaref, 1963.

(17) ——— : La passion d'al-Ḥallāj et l'ordre des Ḥallādjiyyah. (OM 2 : 9—17).

(18) ———: Al-Ḥallāj, le phantasme crucifié des docètes et Satan selon les Yézidis. (OM 2 : 18—28).

(19) ——— : "Ana al-Ḥaqq." Etude historique et critique sur une formule dogmatique de théologie mystique, d'après les sources Islamiques. (OM 2 : 31—9).

(20) ——— : Nouveaux documents persans concernants al-Ḥallāj. (OM 2 : 40—5).

(21) ——— : La survie d'al-Ḥallāj ; tableau chronologique de son influence après sa mort. (OM 2 : 46—60).

(22) ——— : Les études sur les "Isnād" on Chaines de témoignage fondamentales dans la tradition musulmane. (OM 2 : 61—92).

(23) ——— : Etude sur une courbe personelle de vie : le cas de Ḥallāj, martyr mystique de l'Islam. (OM 2 : 167—90).

(24) ——— : La légende de Ḥallācé Mansur en pays turcs. (OM 2 : 93—139).

(25) ——— : L'oeuvre ḥallagienne d'Attar. (OM 2 : 140—66).

(26) ———: Nouvelle bibliographie ḥallagienne. (OM 2 : 191—220).

(27) Massignon, Louis : El-Ḥallāj, mystique de l'Islam. (OM 2 : 221—5).

(28) ——— : Interférences philosophiques et percées métaphysiques dans la mystique ḥallagienne : notion de "l'Essential Désir." (OM 2 : 226—53).

(29) ——— : Qissat Ḥusayn al-Hallādj. (OM 2 : 287—304).

(30) ——— : Le martyr de Ḥallāj à Bagdad. (OM 2 : 272—86).

(31) ——— : L'expérience musulmane de la compassion, ordonnée à l'universal ; à propos de Fātima, et de Ḥallāg. (OM 3 : 642—53).

(32) ——— : Perspective transhistorique sur la vie de Ḥallāj. (OM 2 : 321—42).

(33) ——— : Le Yézidis du Mont Sindjar, "Adorateurs d'Iblis". (OM 2 : 29—30).

(34) ——— : La Guerre Sainte suprême de l'Islam arabe. (OM 2 : 305—20).

(35) ——— : Ibn Sab'īn, et la "conspiration ḥallāgiene" en Andalousie et en Orient au XIIIe siècle, in : Etudes d'Orientalisme Lévi-Provençal, Paris, 1962, vol. II, 661—81.

(36) ——— : Al-Ḥallāj, in : A History of Muslim Philosophy. Ed. M.M. Sharif, vol. I, Wiesbaden, 1963, 346—9.

(37) ———: al-Ḥallādj, in : The Encyclopaedia of Islam. New edition. Vol. III, Leiden/ London, 1971, 99—104.

(38) Mokri, M. : Le chasseur de Dieu et le Mythe

du Roi Higle. Wiesbaden, 1967.

(39) Molé, M. : Les mystiques musulmans. Paris : Presses universitaires de France, 1965.

(40) Nicholson, R.A. : Hallāj, in : Encyclopaedia of Religion and Ethics, vol. VI, 4th Impr., New York 1959 (1913), 480—2.

(41) Nywia, Paul : "Nouveaux fragments inédits de Hallāj", in : Mélanges de la faculté orientale de l'Université St. Joseph de Beyrouth, 62 (1966), 221—44.

(42) O'Leary, De L. : "Al-Hallaj" in : Philosophy East and West, I (1951), 56—62.

(43) Paquignon, P. : "Deux anecdotes sur al-Hallaj", in : Revue du monde musulman (Paris), 7 (1909), 428—32.

(44) Rawan Ferhadi : "Le Majlis de Mansūr-e-Hallāj, de Shams-e-Tabrezi et du Mollā de Roum", in : Revue de études Islamiques (Paris), 23 (1955), 69—91.

(45) Sarrūf, Mlle : Thesis on Ḥallāj, American University of Beirut, Dec. 1956 (under M. Hâyek).

(46) Schimmel, A. : "The martyr-mystic Ḥallāj in Sindhi folk-poetry. Notes on a mystical symbol," in : Numen, (Leiden), 9 (1962), 161—200.

(47) ——— : Al-Halladsch. Maertyrer der Gottesliebe. Leben und Legende ; ausgewaehlt, uebersetzt und eingeleitet von A. S., Koeln : Verlag Jakob Hegner, 1968.

(48) Schimmel, A. : "Mystic Impact of Hallaj," in : Iqbal. Poet-Philosopher of Pakistan. Ed. Hafeez Malik, New York/London, 1971, 310—24.

(49) ——— : Gabriel's Wing. Leiden : Brill, 1963.

(50) ———: "Iqbal and Hallaj", in: Mohammad Iqbal. Pakistan German Forum, Karachi, 1960, 99—111.

(51) ——— : "Zur Verwendung des Halladj-Motives in der indo-persischen Poesie," in : Festschrift H. Corbin. Teheran, in print.

(52) ——— : Mystical Dimensions of Islam. The University of North Carolina Press, Chapel Hill, 1975, 62—77.

(53) Thompson, O. H. : "Al-Hallaj, Saint and Martyr", in : The Muslim World, 19 (1929), 385—402.

عربی :

(۱) عبدالرحمٰن بدوی : "شخصیات خلقه فی الاسلام" ، قاہرہ ۱۹۴۶ع ، ۵۹—۹۱ -

(۲) محمود عبدالحلیم : "التصوف الاسلامی ، شخصیات و نصوص" ، قاہرہ : دارالشرق الغربی ، ۱۹۶۸ع -

(۳) طہ عبدالباقی سرور : "الحسین بن منصور الحلاج ، شہید التصوف الاسلامی" ، طبع ثانی ، قاہرہ ، ۱۹۶۹ع ، ص ۲۳۴ -

(۴) میشال فرید غریب : "الحلاج أو وضوء السلام" ، بیروت ، بلا تاریخ ، ص ۱۴۸ -

(۵) عزّالدین مدنی : الحلّاج رحلة مسرحية"، تونس : مؤسسه عبداللہ ابن عبداللہ ، ۱۹۷۳ع ، صفحات ۹۶ -
(۶) الدکتور محمد غلاب : "التنسک الاسلامی - منشؤه و تطوّره و مذاهبه و رجاله" ، قاہره ، ۱۹۷۰ع ، ص ۱۱۷–۱۳۰ -

فارسی :

(۱) محمد استعلامی : "حلاج" ، تہران ، ۲۵۳۵ -
(۲) محمد حسین رکن زاده : "آدمیت : دانشمندان و سخن سرایان فارس" ، تہران ۱۳۳۸ ، جلد دوم ، ص ۳۳۵–۳۷۵ -
(۳) عبدالغفور روان فرہادی : "حلّاج" ، کابل ، ۱۹۵۱–۱۹۵۲ع -

ترکی :

(۱) احمد کرمیانی (م - ۸۰۵ھ) : "داستان منصور" ، مخطوطه پیرس -
(۲) مریدی (م - ۱۰۰۴ھ) : "منصور نامۂ حلّاج" (قلمی) -
(۳) محمد نیازی مصری (م - ۱۱۰۵ھ) : "منصور بغدادی" ، ۱۲۶۱ھ ، ص ۳۹ -
(۴) صالح زکی اکتای : "حلّاج منصور" ، استانبول ، ۱۹۴۲ع ، ص ۱۱۱ -

اردو :

(۱) "منصور نامہ" (قلمی) ، مصنف فیاض ، تاریخ تصنیف ۱۱۸۵ھ ، مخزونہ کتاب خانہ نواب سالار جنگ -
(۲) "منصور نامہ" (قلمی) ، مصنف دل ، سنہٴ کتابت ۱۲۴۴ھ ، مخزونہ کتاب خانہ نواب سالار جنگ -
(۳) "منصور نامہ" (قلمی) ، مصنف کبیر ، سنہٴ کتابت ۱۲۸۱ھ ، مخزونہ کتاب خانہ نواب سالار جنگ -
(۴) "منصور نامہ" (قلمی) و "نزهة العاشقین" (قلمی) ، مصنف سیّد شاہ حسین ذوق الملقب بہ بحرالعرفان ، معاصر اورنگ زیب عالمگیر -
(۵) احمد علی شیوراجپوری : "قصۂ منصور" (منظوم) ، کانپور : مصطفائی پریس ، ۱۸۵۱ع ، ص ۲۰ -

(٦) نصرت علی : "کلمات الحق" (منظوم) ، دہلی ۱۸۷۰ع -

(۷) اختر نظامی نیاز الہ آبادی : "سیرت حضرت منصور" ، دہلی ، سنہ ندارد ، ص ۱۲۵ -

(۸) عبدالحئی مخلص : "رد البہتان علی الشیخ المنصور الحلّاج" ، لاہور : اسلامیہ اسٹیم پریس ، سنہ ندارد ، ص ۳۲ -

(۹) میر نثار علی شہرت : "سوانح عمری منصور ابن حلّاج" ، لاہور ، سنہ ندارد ، ص ۳۲ -

(۱۰) مولانا ظفر احمد عثمانی : "القول المنصور" ، زیر نگرانی مولانا اشرف علی تھانوی ، طبع جدید ، کراچی ، ۱۹۷۷ع -

(۱۱) رئیس احمد جعفری : "تاریخ تصوف اسلام" ، لاہور : ۱۹۵۰ع ، ص ۲۳۶—۲۵۱ -

(۱۲) مولانا عبدالباری ندوی : "تجدید تصوف و سلوک" ، طبع سوم ، کراچی ، ۱۹۶۲ع ، ص ۲۸۶—۲۹۴ -

(۱۳) کیپٹن واحد بخش سیال : "مشاہدۂ حق" ، کراچی ، ۱۹۷۴ع ، ص ۱۵۷—۱۶۴ ، ۱۷۲ -

سندھی :

محمد صالح بھٹی : "منصور حلّاج" ، حیدرآباد سندھ ، ۱۹۵۲ع -

پشتو :

ملّا غلام احمد : "قصۂ منصور حلّاج" ، پشاور ، ۱۲۹۴ھ/ ۱۸۷۷ع -

بنگالی :

مزمل حق : "مہارشی منصور" ، کلکتہ : ۱۸۹۶ع ، طبع ہشتم ۱۹۴۵ع ، ص ۱۲۸ -